Carbon Done Correctly

Carbon Done Correctly

A Model for Climate Mitigation from the Global South to Wall Street

Unsung Heroes Fighting Climate Change

By Richard H. Lawrence, Jr.
with James E. Hackett

HARRIMAN HOUSE LTD
3 Viceroy Court
Bedford Road
Petersfield
Hampshire
GU32 3LJ
GREAT BRITAIN

Tel: +44 (0)1730 233870
Email: enquiries@harriman-house.com
Website: harriman.house

First published in 2024.
Copyright © Richard H. Lawrence, Jr.

The right of Richard H. Lawrence, Jr. to be identified as the Author has been asserted in accordance with the Copyright, Design and Patents Act 1988.

Hardback ISBN: 978-1-80409-061-9
eBook ISBN: 978-1-80409-062-6

British Library Cataloguing in Publication Data
A CIP catalogue record for this book can be obtained from the British Library.

This book is produced from independently certified FSC paper to ensure responsible forest management.

If readers would like to offset their emissions, they can do so at www.cooleffect.org

Printed and bound by CPI Group (UK) Ltd, Croydon, CR0 4YY

This book is dedicated to Siddharth "Sid" Yadav, a loved and respected colleague and one of the great carbon accounting experts of the world. He recognized that climate change would disproportionately impact disadvantaged communities, and he dedicated his life to helping the Global South by bringing integrity to the Voluntary Carbon Market.

Contents

Contributors

The following is a list of those who have brought their stories to life in this book. There are many more whose contributions to climate change mitigation cannot be described within our scope and we express our gratitude for their dedication.

Esther Adams, Carbon Program Director, Proyecto Mirador

David Antonioli, Former Chief Executive Officer, Verra

Sandeep Roy Choudhury, Co-Founder & Director, VNV Advisory Services

Arne Fjørtoft, Co-Founder & Chief Executive Officer, Worldview International Foundation

Patrick Flynn, Former Senior Vice President & Global Head of Sustainability, Salesforce

Emilia Giron de Mendoza, Executive Director, Proyecto Mirador

Jeremy Grantham, Co-Founder & Trustee, The Grantham Foundation for the Protection of the Environment

Dharsono Hartono, Founder & President Director, PT Rimba Makmur Utama

John Holdren, Research Professor, Harvard University, Kennedy School of Government

Alexia Kelly, Managing Director, Carbon Policy & Markets Initiative, High Tide Foundation; former Netflix sustainability executive

Mark Kenber, Executive Director, Voluntary Carbon Markets Integrity Initiative

Dee Lawrence, Director, Cool Effect

Skye ("Cielo") Lawrence, Chief Product Officer, Biome Analytics

Jodi Manning, Vice President, Corporate Partnerships, Cool Effect

Sonia Medina, Executive Director, Climate Change, Children's Investment Fund Foundation

Elder Mendoza Mejia, Director of Operations, Proyecto Mirador

Rafael Mendoza Giron, Director of International Operations, Proyecto Mirador

Juan Carlos Guzmán, Leader of Team Ghostbusters, Proyecto Mirador

Annette Nazareth, Chair, Integrity Council for the Voluntary Carbon Market

Fredy Pineda, *Ejecutor*, Proyecto Mirador

Sassan Saatchi, Senior Research Scientist, NASA Jet Propulsion Laboratory; Chief Executive Officer, C-Trees.org

Robbie Schingler, Co-Founder & Chief Strategy Officer, Planet Labs

Lisa Shibata, Director of Sustainability, Chipotle Mexican Grill

Stevan Simich, Founder & Chief Executive Officer, Mogli Technologies

Dean Still, Director, Aprovecho Research Center

Introduction:
We Have Had A
Great Run, But...

"There are no silver bullets, only silver buckshot."

—Bill McKibben

THE WORLD HAS experienced 140 years of economic progress that has brought billions of people out of poverty and modernized lifestyles around the globe.

We have so much to celebrate: science solving cancer and other diseases; iPhones, chatbots, methane-detecting satellites; prosthetics to replace hips and knees. We have heat in the winters and air conditioning in the summers; and, sometimes, a little whiskey with friends.

Logically and predictably, while working toward all these developments, our economic systems incentivized us to use the lowest-cost energy sources. This had an unintended side effect on our planet.

Too much carbon dioxide (CO_2) was released, at zero cost to emitters.

Economists call CO_2 emissions an externality, or a cost that is not priced. Examples include pollution from factories, second-hand smoke, and

1

biodiversity loss from deforestation. The biggest externality of all is the CO_2 emitted into the atmosphere.

For the first 100 years of this 140-year economic boom, there was no scientific awareness, let alone consensus, about the unintended consequences of our reliance on fossil fuels. It wasn't until 1977, when Exxon's scientists raised the flag of potential "catastrophic consequences" from rising CO_2 concentrations in the atmosphere, that people started to take the early warnings by Dr. James Hansen and others more seriously.

Fast forward to 2023, and the science is abundantly clear. Our emissions are warming the atmosphere and causing global climate disruptions at a scale that is hard for any of us to deny. We have experienced fires, floods, hurricanes, typhoons, and record heat. We have learned about the acidification of our oceans, the melting of the Greenland ice sheet, the bleaching of coral reefs, and so much more.

If we are to continue to deliver broad-based economic growth to the eight billion people living on this planet, the objective is clear. We must limit carbon dioxide and methane emissions while continuing to deliver equitable economic growth and social benefits to the citizens of Earth.

Now, we need action on all fronts

There is no value in assigning blame. What's done is done. It is time to move forward. With the same ingenuity that created so much advancement in the past, we must now turn our talents to fixing the problem we have created.

And we must do so with urgency. This problem will not wait. Delaying our response—or worse, doing nothing—exposes humanity, particularly the most disadvantaged communities, to the risk of a climate catastrophe and the economic and social devastation it will cause.

We also need to recognize that there is no silver bullet to resolve the problem of CO_2 concentrations in the atmosphere. We need to utilize all the tools in our toolbox to reverse carbon emissions from our economic systems. We need compostable plastics and the infrastructure to support their safe disposal; high-resolution satellites to pinpoint methane leaks; green hydrogen; new generations of nuclear plants; environmentally safe energy storage systems; and many new technologies that are not yet commercially viable or have not even been invented.

We need an "all of the above" solution.

The Voluntary Carbon Market

One of the essential tools in our toolbox is the Voluntary Carbon Market (VCM). The VCM is not *the* solution; it is *a* solution. The VCM represents one tool in the "all of the above" toolbox.

Our analysis has confirmed that we cannot reach 1.5 degrees, and corporations cannot reach their Net Zero commitments, without the VCM. This is why so many of us are dedicated to creating the Framework for the VCM. The VCM is an essential tool to fight climate change.

An overview of the VCM

What is the VCM?

The Voluntary Carbon Market is a system where companies and individuals can purchase carbon credits to offset their greenhouse gas emissions. These carbon credits are generated from projects that reduce or remove carbon dioxide or other greenhouse gases from the atmosphere.

The VCM can deliver benefits for the planet because:

- It puts a price on carbon to communicate the cost of carbon emissions— an essential element of integrating the true costs of climate pollution into the global economy.

- It enables corporates to immediately complement their efforts to reduce operational carbon emissions, increasing their ambition and impact.

- It is a market mechanism that can advance essential ecosystem restoration, support critical biodiversity, reduce air pollution, increase climate resilience, and improve social outcomes for disadvantaged communities, particularly in the Global South.

- It is a platform to mobilize billions of dollars of private capital into projects that reduce carbon emissions and accelerate the energy transition that would otherwise not have occurred.

The learning curve

The conceptual overview of the VCM is useful, but to really understand the VCM, we need to dig deeper. We need to understand more about carbon projects, and what it takes to create high-quality projects that verifiably contribute to the fight against climate change.

An analogy to investing in the stock market is helpful: an investor must be able to judge a company's performance to make a rational investment decision. This is no less true for the VCM, but the fact is that creating great carbon projects, which were virtually non-existent at the beginning of this century, and the analysis by buyers to differentiate between carbon projects, are skills that are still evolving. We are still on the learning curve.

The ultimate objective is for all market participants—carbon projects and corporate buyers—to work exclusively in high-quality, high-integrity carbon credits. We call this the Top of the Pyramid, where the highest level of integrity and quality is the law of the land.

In the first sections of this book we share the story of Proyecto Mirador, a non-profit established in 2004 to help disadvantaged communities in rural Honduras. We tell the story of how, from humble beginnings, Proyecto Mirador forged the path to success as a leading carbon mitigation project in Central America. We hope that the lessons learned at Proyecto Mirador may help others as they strive to reach the Top of the Pyramid.

We then tell the story of Cool Effect, a non-profit created in 2014 to connect carbon projects with corporations seeking to offset their carbon emissions in the Voluntary Carbon Market. The Cool Effect business model offers insight on what is needed, by both buyers and sellers, to reach the Top of the Pyramid in the VCM.

These experiences, at both Proyecto Mirador and Cool Effect, illuminate both the huge potential of the VCM to mitigate climate change, and the actions that will be required for the VCM to reach maturity.

A Framework for the VCM

In the final section of the book, we discuss how improvements must be made, and weaknesses rectified, for the Voluntary Carbon Market to play its essential role in the fight against climate change. The VCM is a relatively new financial market, and any new market faces trial and error in its formative stages. But time is of the essence, and we must work urgently. This book therefore proposes a framework to improve and strengthen the VCM to accelerate its advancement as a fully functional financial market.

Underlying every aspect of the VCM Framework that we propose here is transparency. Without full transparency, the VCM cannot succeed; with transparency, everything is possible. Transparency determines success for the VCM, so much so that it can be described as a maxim:

Transparency leads to Trust;

Trust leads to Scale;

and with Scale, the VCM becomes a financial asset class.

In 2021, the Voluntary Carbon Market reached $2 billion, four times its size in 2020. That is impressive and good news, but it is a tiny fraction of what it needs to be. The VCM needs to reach scale in the global financial markets if it is to achieve its full potential.

Voices from the Top of the Pyramid

If there is reason for optimism in the fight to mitigate climate change, it can be found in the emotional stories of the unsung leaders on the front lines to reduce carbon emissions. The amazing creativity of humanity is on display every day in the many people out there working for positive change.

This book incorporates the voices of leaders from all sectors of the VCM who are striving to get to the Top of the Pyramid, including the following:

- An 85-year-old Norwegian who figured out that communities protected by mangroves survived the 2004 tsunami in the Indian Ocean. He also learned that mangrove trees, by sequestering CO_2, were a climate-saving miracle tree, and he has planted 75 million mangrove trees in the years since the tsunami—all funded by carbon credits.

- A mother of three with no prior work experience, but with exceptional innate talent, who has led an organization to build over 330,000 fuel-efficient stoves for the poorest of the poor in Honduras and Guatemala—also funded by carbon credits.

- Three sustainability officers for Fortune 200 companies who, with vision and determination, set their companies on a path to Net Zero.

- A successful investor and philanthropist who first raised the alarm within the investment industry to the dangers of our changing climate.

———————

In the following pages, our journey to the Top of the Pyramid begins, oddly, with a weak storm moving slowly across the Atlantic Ocean.

PART ONE

Hurricane Mitch Creates Proyecto Mirador

Prologue

"We were all covering the election, and I don't think we were paying proper attention to the storm."

—Ted Koppel, Anchor, ABC Nightline

I T WAS MID-OCTOBER, 1998. A seasonal storm system was reportedly forming and making its way westward from the coast of Africa, but so far, the storm was disorganized and weak. Coming so late in the year, it was not anticipated to become much of a threat.

However, by the time the storm reached the south-eastern Caribbean on October 22, it was designated a tropical storm and given the name Mitch. Within 48 hours, Mitch strengthened to a Category 1 hurricane. Meteorologists began to take notice. Then, incredibly and unexpectedly, Mitch strengthened to Category 5. The center of the storm was still at sea, but the outer bands of Mitch's massive reach engulfed Honduras with fierce wind and rain.

Forecasters expected the storm to continue north on a path into the Gulf of Mexico, and it appeared that the worst of the storm would bypass Honduras. But then, full of surprises, on October 29, Mitch reversed course. The storm's full, destructive brunt roared onto Honduras's north coast with overwhelming rain, winds of over 150 miles per hour, and a 12-foot storm surge.

It would have been a historically devastating storm for Honduras under any circumstances. Still, Mitch's worst cruelty was that it stalled as it made landfall, crawled in the slowest and longest possible route across the country, and pummeled Honduras not for hours but for a week.

Thirty-six inches of rain fell, and unofficial reports in some locations recorded 75 inches. Rivers and streams flooded like tsunamis, washing out 60% of the roads and bridges, destroying 70% of the crops, and killing more than 7,000 people as houses and buildings were swept away. Wind flattened everything. The airport in San Pedro Sula was 21 feet under water. Mudslides buried entire villages. Sudden homelessness was rampant. The toll was catastrophic. Hurricane Mitch was a total reset for Honduras. It has been said that the hurricane destroyed 50 years of economic progress.

People were completely isolated in the remote agricultural villages where most Hondurans live. Food was running out, potable water was scarce, and disease was spreading. In these rural communities—all of them poor— local governments did not have the resources to cope. Federal government aid was limited and slow to mobilize, so there was no trickle-down from Tegucigalpa, the capital of Honduras.

To make matters worse, midterm elections in the U.S. were coming down to the wire, and the media paid scant attention to Mitch. When foreign aid finally reached Honduran shores, the infrastructure was obliterated, so there was no way to get that aid to most of the rural population. Communities were isolated and tens of thousands of people were stranded.

Ramon Villeda Morales International Airport, San Pedro Sula, 21 feet under water (1998).

The Medical Mission in Atima, Honduras

"You don't lose if you get knocked down; you lose if you stay down."

—Muhammad Ali

An opportunity to help

MY FAMILY AND I wanted to help Honduras, but we weren't sure how. The opportunity came in 2001 when a friend introduced me to The Organization for Community Health Outreach (OCHO), a group of medical professionals out of Baltimore. OCHO was establishing a medical mission to Atima, a small town in the mountainous region of northwestern Honduras, to be staffed with 20 American doctors, supported by an equal number of volunteer high school students and four or five chaperones. Volunteers were needed. My daughter Skye and I talked our way into the Mission as the only non-Baltimorean members.

When we arrived at Atima in June 2001, the story of Hurricane Mitch was still unfolding. The evidence was plain to see. Many roads were still washed out. Homes and buildings were still under repair. Some damaged structures remained abandoned. Transportation was difficult, and sometimes, further out into the surrounding hills, impossible even for pickup trucks.

Plus, another kind of hurricane

Atima, a town of about 10,000 people, is located high in the Honduran hills, and the altitude and climate are perfect for growing coffee. Coffee was the region's main export crop and the most important source of employment and income. The problem for Atima was that now, when cash from coffee exports was so desperately needed, coffee prices had crashed.

All commodity markets, including coffee, are cyclical, and the boom-and-bust cycles make sustained progress for developing countries difficult. But this depression in the coffee cycle was different; it was much worse. With the rising popularity of coffee in China in the early 1990s, demand for coffee boomed. That was initially good news for coffee growers, but worldwide coffee supplies—propelled by free trade globalization—had surged so much that by 2001, coffee prices had fallen by 85%. At precisely the moment that Honduras needed the coffee price to be high, it was so low that the cost of harvesting coffee exceeded the income it produced. This was another kind of hurricane for Honduras: an economic one.

These people needed help.

Treating 1,500 people a day

On our first day in Atima, we transformed the town's only elementary school into a medical clinic. What available space remained in the school was used as a dormitory for medical mission staff. We had to work quickly because the clinic would open its doors early the following morning.

The sight outside the clinic that next morning was stunning. Rumors of the clinic—with its U.S. doctors and U.S. medications—had preceded our arrival, and a huge crowd had gathered outside the front gate. There were people everywhere! People from remote villages with names not found on maps. Worried mothers, all so young—and babies, babies, and more babies. The sense of desperation was visible on their faces as they pushed their way into the clinic through the front gate. They never complained, but there were many pleas for help, some spoken, some just seen in their eyes.

Inside, we did what we could to organize the elementary school into a functioning medical clinic. Educational material hung on classroom walls: world maps, alphabets, math tables, and crayon drawings. Doctors and patients sat at low stools and tables sized for young children. But it worked, and we treated nearly 1,500 patients a day.

The range of conditions confronted was head-spinning. There were gastrointestinal issues caused by unclean drinking water; viral and bacterial infections; dental issues; wounds and burns; gynecological afflictions and pregnancies; impetigo and scabies; and chronic respiratory problems.

The clinic had brought stocks of medicines and clothes. Medications were always in short supply in rural Honduras, and desperately so after Hurricane Mitch. For the local people, the medicines were a godsend. Mothers would tell us they had every illness on earth, not to lie purposefully but because they knew their families would need those drugs at some point and they had no idea if we would ever return.

The men would show up late in the afternoon on their way home from working in the fields. These were strong men with hardly any formal education but with great integrity. One couldn't help but be drawn to them. Many suffered from shoulder pain from years of machete use, or needed glasses to correct poor eyesight. Some of them simply needed shoes.

Also, members of the medical mission staff—doctors, translators, and students—were also getting sick, primarily with intestinal issues. We maintained a daily count of how many were down so we could reallocate enough staff to cover the work.

Our home sweet home in Atima

When our work at the clinic wound down to a close in the evening, we were physically exhausted and emotionally drained. We needed rest at the end of those days. Instead, we made do with our makeshift dormitory. I am not complaining: we were there for the medical clinic, not the comforts. We can laugh about it now.

We rigged up makeshift showers in the playground outside. Cold water! There were six toilets for our group of 45, and we never knew how many would be functioning at any one time. We slept in classrooms on concrete floors in tents with sleeping bags. Hard concrete floors. Those who snored were politely directed to a separate classroom. The students had their own two rooms because they talked and laughed too much for us sleepy adults. And somehow, exhausted from long days at the clinic, we slept soundly, at least until crowing roosters woke us. Morning already? It can't be; it is still dark. Look at your watch. 3:00 AM! You have got to be kidding. Don't roosters crow at dawn? Not in Honduras.

But none of that mattered. We were here for the medical mission; our work was important and rewarding. These people needed our help, and we had skills and supplies that were otherwise completely absent from Atima in 2001. Our work for these people was the only thing that mattered.

Patients waiting outside the medical clinic in Atima.

"Dad! I figured it out!"

"Some of the greatest things… have come about by serendipity, the greatest discoveries."

—Alan Alda

A PERSISTENT COUGH WAS among the most common ailments we treated at the medical clinic. Women and children were the most affected, and the cause was a mystery. The doctors gave them nebulizers and they sat along the wall, mask to face, breathing deeply. The nebulizers were in constant use.

The doctors determined it was not a bacterial or viral infection, so it had to be environmental. But the air in this mountainous region was clean, there were few vehicles to create pollution, and people couldn't afford cigarettes.

It didn't make sense that so many people were afflicted. What was causing this?

It was 2003 and we were on our third annual visit to Atima. My daughter Skye was 14 and the youngest member of the medical mission's Youth Group. A fair-haired gringa, small in stature but with outsized enthusiasm, Skye was especially popular with the young girls in the village. Skye's name, which honors her ancestors from the Isle of Skye in Scotland, translates in Spanish as Cielo. Once her local friends made the connection, Skye, to them, was ever after called Cielo.

15

One late afternoon, at the end of a long day at the clinic, a group of young girls came by and asked Cielo to join them. It was that time of day when workers returned from the fields, women were busy preparing dinner, and young children were free to play. Cielo and her friends ran off together as we tended to the last patients and readied the clinic to close.

Later, with our work done for the day, I went outside to sit on a bench in the schoolyard for a few quiet moments. I looked up to see Cielo, who had just visited a house in the village, running toward the clinic and waving excitedly.

The typical house in Atima, as in all rural Honduras, is one story, made of adobe blocks or cement bricks, with a tin roof. Behind the house is a pozo (water tub) for washing dishes, clothes, and just about everything else. A stack of firewood lines the wall. Further back in the yard is an outhouse and perhaps a few fruit trees. Chickens, pigs, and dogs roam freely. Inside the house is one open room with a sleeping area separated by a cloth or plastic sheet hung from the ceiling. The remaining space is used as a living area, largely given over to a cooking area, table, and stools. Floors are either cement or just packed earth.

Cooking is done on the traditional *fogón*, an open-fire cookstove typically consisting of an oil drum lid or simple steel cooktop placed over a circular adobe frame with a large opening through which fuelwood is fed. The stoves burn seven or eight hours daily, simmering corn mash for tortillas, cooking beans and rice, or heating up coffee. Some houses have tin chimneys running vertically up to the ceiling, some have diagonal chimneys running outside, and some have—my favorite—a horizontal chimney with less than a 50/50 chance of removing smoke from the house. These chimneys are mostly ineffectual, and much of the smoke remains inside as a harsh, grey haze. The walls and ceiling become blackened with soot from constant smoke. When Cielo entered her friend's house that afternoon, the smoke made her eyes water and caused her to cough.

And so it was that, as I was sitting outside the clinic late that afternoon, Cielo ran through the front gate and shouted, "Dad! I figured it out! The nebulizers! It's the stoves!"

Treat the cause, not the symptoms

At the medical clinic, the nebulizers were treating the respiratory symptoms of wood smoke inhalation, but how could we eliminate the cause of the illness, these open-fire stoves? How do you solve the problem of indoor air pollution? How significant was the problem of bad stoves in Atima? Did bad stoves exist across Honduras? Initially, we had no answers to these questions.

Through more and more conversations, we confirmed that every home in Atima used inefficient wood-burning cookstoves, and indeed the existence of lung disease occurred across rural Honduras. These inefficient, unhealthy stoves have been used for centuries. The problem was endemic.

Serendipity, again

Three months later, back home in the United States, my wife, Dee, mentioned excitedly at dinner that she had heard a story on NPR about a stove called La Justa that was designed to burn wood efficiently and used a chimney to vent smoke from the house. We dropped our forks. Just as Cielo had, by good chance, discovered the problem of the stoves, serendipity had presented a possible solution.

We learned that the La Justa stove was being installed in Honduras by a non-profit group called AHDESA, run by Ignacio "Nacho" Osorto, in association with Trees, Water & People in Fort Collins, Colorado, led by Stuart Conway. We contacted Stuart, who introduced us to Don Nacho. We described our work in Atima and our observations of respiratory illness and stove smoke. AHDESA had been installing La Justa stoves in Honduras for three years to address the threat of deforestation, not indoor air pollution. They enthusiastically agreed to help us. Don Nacho offered to send one of his key employees, Don Beltran Amador, to meet us on our next trip to get us started. Cielo took the initiative and raised enough money from family and friends to build 29 stoves.

Building the first 29 stoves

That following summer, Don Beltran met us in Atima. Our team comprised Cielo, me, a few gringos eager to escape the medical clinic, and two local men, Chepe and Santos, to work with us as stove builders. Don Beltran, a believer in on-the-job training, put us straight to work.

We worked inside the homes, scavenged around backyards for critical materials, cut bricks with machetes, mixed cement, measured the dimensions of the stove, and used mud to tie together the adobe blocks that served as a frame. No one ever had a lousy day building stoves with the Hondurans. At the end of the day, Don Beltran would have two spots of mud on his shoes while the gringos were covered from head to toe. We all shared smiles.

At the end of that week of building 29 stoves, while standing near the central square of Atima, I asked Don Beltran, "How many stoves do we need to build to resolve the issue of indoor air pollution in Atima and the nearby villages?" Beltran raised his eyes to the surrounding hills, did a 360-degree turn, pondered a second or two, and said, "500." My jaw dropped.

Don Beltran teaching a homeowner how to maintain her new stove.

500 Stoves! How? Who?

Building those first 29 stoves had felt like a major accomplishment. But 500 stoves? How could we possibly build 500 stoves? Chepe and Santos couldn't handle that alone. We would need leadership. We would need to be organized. I could help, but I had my day job, family, responsibilities, and commitments. We needed someone local with the determination and integrity to manage our stove-building ambitions. We needed someone who could get things done. We needed an exceptional person, someone with talent.

We needed Doña Emilia. In the next chapter, we introduce you to this extraordinary woman.

Elderly woman bathed in the smoke of her traditional *fogón* cookstove.

Meeting Doña Emilia

"When I am told that something is difficult, I have always said, 'Yes, it doesn't matter, we will do it.'"

—Doña Emilia Giron de Mendoza,
Executive Director, Proyecto Mirador

I MET DOÑA EMILIA Mendoza on the first day of our first trip to Atima in 2001. She greeted us on arrival and helped us get situated in the elementary school that would serve as our clinic and dormitory. "But first," she said, "you are probably all hungry from your journey to Honduras." She showed us the house down the dirt street where our meals would be served.

Amidst the crush of serving meals to as many as 40 of us at once, one could not help but be immediately drawn to Doña Emilia. There was something about her that one instinctively recognized—her calm efficiency, her gentle guidance, her easy smile. She always seemed to have things at hand. She was clearly the leader in the house, the *jefa*, but in an understated, quietly confident way. The operation to prepare, serve and clean up meals for 40 people ran like clockwork under her guidance.

I was not alone in recognizing Doña Emilia's capabilities. I noticed that others would come to the house to ask Doña Emilia for advice on an issue or help to get something done. With Atima working hard to recover from the devastation caused by Hurricane Mitch, Doña Emilia's ability to get things done and her quickness to find solutions were unmatched.

Credit where credit is due

The international offices of the Episcopal Church sponsored our medical mission in Atima. It was represented locally by Doña Emilia's husband, Padre Jose Luis Mendoza, pastor of nearly 30 local Episcopal congregations across Santa Bárbara Province.

Padre Jose Luis, an engaging man with an easy laugh, recognized the need for the medical clinic in Atima and arranged to locate the clinic in the local elementary school. And while his pastoral duties kept him extremely busy, often traveling about the region's towns and villages, it was Doña Emilia, we quickly understood, whose volunteered effort made this medical mission a day-to-day success. She arranged our housing and meals, coordinated the delivery of supplies and equipment, spread the word about the clinic to the remote villages around Atima, and found transportation to the clinic for the sick and elderly. She did all of this behind the scenes, never seeking or accepting credit.

One example from the early days of the clinic stands out. The clinic was such a success that crowding immediately became an overwhelming problem. Large groups of people gathered outside on the street, jostling and disordered, in the heat of the tropical sun. We needed help to keep up. On seeing this, Doña Emilia organized local communities to schedule dedicated times for each village: Tuesday morning for Berlin, Tuesday afternoon for San Pedrito, and so on. And she took the initiative to arrange for people to wait sequentially in the cool shelter of the nearby Episcopal church. Waiting times fell, medical care improved, and we could treat more patients than ever before.

Doña Emilia, I recognized, with barely more than a high school education and no outside work experience beyond her home and family, was an exceptional and gifted woman. There was no telling what she could accomplish if given a chance.

Making hopes possible

And so it was, when faced with the challenge to build 500 stoves, that I sat with Doña Emilia for a cup of coffee. The story of that meeting is best told by Doña Emilia herself:

> I sat in a coffee shop with Don Ricardo in 2004 when he told me about the possibility of working on the stove project with Mirador. This was at the time when the first stoves had been built. The people were interested in the project, and many more were asking for stoves. Don Ricardo asked, "Will you help me build 500 stoves in the Atima Valley?" I didn't know what I was facing, but I agreed. I wanted to help.
>
> I felt the same then as I did a few years earlier when I was asked if I would help the medical mission. "Can you receive a group of so many people?" they asked, and I said I could. "But it is a very big group." I still said, "Yes, it's okay." I have never been afraid to say the opposite when I am told something is difficult. I have always said "Yes, it doesn't matter; we will do it." That's how it was when I sat with Don Ricardo. Building 500 stoves would be challenging, but I told him, "Yes, we will do it."

Less than a month later, Doña Emilia could be found driving a second-hand Land Cruiser through the small communities dotted across the mountains above Atima, at work convincing ladies that Chepe and Santos could build a better stove for them. None of the ladies had the courage to say no to Doña Emilia. Not then, not now.

With Doña Emilia at the wheel, we established a non-profit called Proyecto Mirador. With that, we were in business, albeit a money-losing venture. But much lay ahead for this modest woman. We would eventually build not just 500 stoves, but over 2,000 stoves, in the mountain villages surrounding Atima. Eighteen years later, Doña Emilia is still going strong as we tick over 330,000 stoves built since inception.

There is only one way any of this could have happened. It could only have occurred with Doña Emilia. She gave me the confidence to build stoves in some of the poorest communities in rural Honduras. She is among that special class of people who get things done today and make tomorrow's hopes possible.

Doña Emilia outside the clinic in Atima with waiting patients.

Professor Elder Mendoza

"Dejame probarlo."

"Let me test it."

—Professor Elder Mendoza Mejia,
Director of Operations, Proyecto Mirador

DOÑA EMILIA HAD agreed to help me establish Proyecto Mirador and lead the effort in Honduras to build the next 500 stoves. Let's be clear: the objective to build 500 stoves nearly exceeded our imagination. This would require building an organization, schedules, suppliers, coordination with the community, and bookkeeping—in other words, an operating enterprise.

We didn't have that yet.

We had Doña Emilia in Honduras; and in the U.S., we had me, my daughter, Cielo, my wife, Dee, and my son, Blake. We were in that limbo between believing in an idea and making it a reality.

We took it one step at a time.

Birds of a feather

One of Doña Emilia's first steps was to contact Professor Elder Mendoza. Professor Elder, then a 25-year-old entrepreneur, owned a small metal fabrication plant that made school desks for the government. Could he, Doña Emilia asked, make *planchas*, the cooktops, for our stoves? Professor Elder listened, asked questions, and quickly understood. He offered a fair price and committed to meeting the delivery schedule. Just as I knew that Doña Emilia was the only person to help me run Mirador, Doña Emilia knew that Professor Elder was the only one to help her. Her instincts were correct. Shortly after that, Professor Elder delivered *planchas* that were well-made, on time, and on budget.

Professor Elder, always with a quick wit, insisted on loading the *planchas* into Doña Emilia's Land Cruiser and helping her deliver them to houses. He was polite and patient when explaining the stoves to the homeowners. He also began to observe the construction of stoves, volunteering a helping hand when needed and unobtrusively offering improvements. It was only natural that Doña Emilia eventually offered Professor Elder a full-time job with Mirador; and, just as naturally, Professor Elder accepted.

A man of character

I first met Professor Elder on our next trip to Honduras. He is a big man, powerfully built, with a broad smile. He is immediately engaging. But for all his outsized presence, Professor Elder greets you with a soft handshake that reflects his patient ways, calm confidence, and polite modesty. People are drawn to Professor Elder.

It is a sign of character that Professor Elder, hardworking to a fault, is always the first to pick up the heaviest object in a pile, or to jump at the most challenging task. He is respectful. He never angers. He listens. It is another sign of character that, in the patriarchal society of Honduras, Doña Emilia is Professor Elder's boss, yet, both are free of any macho sensitivities and get on with their work.

Professor Elder, stove tinkerer extraordinaire

Professor Elder is a problem solver at his core, and we had plenty of problems at Mirador in the early years to keep him busy.

Professor Elder is called "Professor" by all because he once taught school in Santa Bárbara. The name fits. He has a keen interest in everything we do, strives to be well-informed, and is always on the lookout to make improvements. When frustrating problems arise, Professor Elder takes charge calmly and methodically and finds solutions. His determination and ability to always find a way inspires confidence.

Having attended a high school run by German engineers, Professor Elder developed an engineer's love of tinkering with materials and designs. How can we make the *plancha* more durable? Is the chimney the weakest part? How can we train technicians better? How should we teach the homeowner? Are the stove dimensions the most efficient? His answer to new ideas or suggestions is always a willing *"Dejame probarlo."* ("Let me test it.") It is fair to say that Professor Elder and his team invented, tested, and approved virtually every improvement to the stove.

In those early years, when we were struggling to create this new venture, my partnership with Doña Emilia and Professor Elder gave Mirador the confidence to keep moving forward. The truth is that the project would not have succeeded without their determination, hard work, and problem solving.

And just as important was the integrity and aspiration they brought to everything they did, inspiring all of us, in Honduras and in California, to keep doing all we could to help them make Mirador the most successful stove project in the Americas.

Professor Elder Mendoza representing Proyecto Mirador
at a climate event.

La Justa

"I like this project. It is the first time anyone has helped us."

—Jose Daniel Soto Hernandez, Mirador Report, June 2019

T HE LA JUSTA stove we installed in Atima in the early 2000s was based on a design from Larry Winiarski, an American engineer who dedicated his life to helping the disadvantaged across the globe.

Using the simple idea of a "rocket" combustion chamber, wood is burned in a small, L-shaped chamber at the front of the stove. Hot air rises inside the stove to heat the cooking surface (the *plancha*). That rising hot air draws in more outside air over the fire, sustaining the flame, cooking the food, and pushing smoke out the chimney. Combustion is nearly 100% complete, meaning more heat from less wood and less smoke, soot, and toxins.

Does it really work?

The technical promise of the La Justa stove sounds great on paper, but it had to work in the real world of rural Honduras. In building the first 29 stoves in Atima, we learned that the stove delivers on its promise:

- As we had hoped, the La Justa stove effectively removed harmful smoke from the house.

• The stove burned less wood.

• Most important, women liked the stove. This is essential. We had one chance to make this work. If women didn't like cooking on the stove, it would fail to catch on.

Designed for local success

The stove also needed to accommodate local practices to succeed in rural Honduras:

• The stove is designed to be easily constructed with local skills and materials. No fancy electronics, imported parts, or PhD-level construction methods are needed, and there are no supply chain challenges. It can be built in less than half a day, it can be operated and maintained by any homeowner, and it will last for more than six years.

• The stove accommodates the Honduran style of cooking. Sometimes this requires a lower temperature for long simmering of beans and corn, or at other times, high heat to rapidly boil water for coffee. And the stove must be durable: it will be used seven hours a day, every day of the year.

• Compared to the old traditional stove, users liked that it lit easily, heated up quickly, and provided variable heat across the *plancha*. They wanted their lungs and houses to be cleaner by eliminating smoke. The La Justa stove earned a welcome place in Honduran homes.

Early La Justa stove under construction.

No Cuesta, No Cuida

Homeowners needed to contribute to the construction of the stove. Requiring a small investment from homeowners makes the stove far more meaningful to them than simply receiving it as a donation. To facilitate this, the folks at AHDESA had developed an innovative co-investment structure.

The homeowner is asked to contribute materials they are likely to have lying around their backyard or that they can inexpensively obtain. These include the stove base, adobe blocks, bricks, a small amount of cement, a few pieces of metal rebar, a used milk powder can, and a bag of wood ash used for insulation. Mirador provides everything else: the know-how, the actual construction, and the *plancha* (cooktop), chimney, and firebox made from six ceramic pieces.

This co-investment, which we call *"No Cuesta, No Cuida,"* literally translates as "No Cost, No Care," meaning that if something doesn't cost you anything, you will not take care of it. Homeowners understood and quickly saw that their small contribution to the stove was also a good investment because it used less wood and saved them time and money.

Using the *No Cuesta, No Cuida* model, we calculated that the payback on the homeowner's investment in the stove was less than a few months. The co-investment by the homeowner and the co-benefits generated by the stove made a green light go on for us. We had to make more stoves.

No Cuesta, No Cuida has been an essential factor in the success of our stove. When homeowners have a sense of ownership in their stove, they will take care of it, take pride in it, and maintain it. Looking back now, we realize that *No Cuesta, No Cuida* was an early step in creating a business model for Mirador.

Benefits of the stove

We were buoyant at Mirador as we entered our fourth year. Led by Doña Emilia and Professor Elder, with technicians hired to help build the stoves, installations expanded so that we were able to reach our goal of 500 stoves in Atima in 2005; and in 2006, stove installations grew to over 1,000. Our objective for 2007 was to reach 2,000 stoves.

There were real benefits of the stove for various groups, as follows:

For homeowners

Mirador was founded on two obvious and essential benefits: primarily, the health benefits of removing smoke from the house; and secondarily, the economic benefits to families from using less wood. We had no scientific measurements to quantify these benefits, but simple observation and positive reports from homeowners proved anecdotally that the stove accomplished those objectives.

For the communities

As we continued our work in Honduras, more and more of the stove's benefits were revealed and became core parts of the Mirador Model.

Mirador employment

As we became more proficient at building stoves, our staff grew accordingly. Over the first few years, we went from one to three, to four, to 30 employees. And these were good jobs.

Family income

Surveys revealed that each stove averaged approximately an 8–11% increase in household income from less wood purchased or time saved collecting wood.

Local businesses

Our supply chain of stove materials grew, creating employment at local family-owned businesses providing us with chimneys, the six ceramic pieces that comprised our firebox, and the *plancha*. Economists have a fancy term for this: the multiplier effect. In Santa Bárbara Province, the people call it good news. We were creating more jobs in Santa Bárbara than any entity other than the government.

Empowerment of women

With less time spent cooking and less time collecting firewood, the stoves were freeing women to do more for their families, their communities, and themselves. This cannot be measured. It is invaluable.

Elderly woman carrying firewood home to feed her cookstove.

In just the first few years, we learned that this simple cookstove was a health intervention that changed people's lives and created income and employment for locals. More than we ever anticipated, the stoves generated benefits across the community. The stoves were proving their worth, fueling our ambition to build more. Solicitations from communities across Honduras began to pour into Mirador's office.

Here are the words of Hondurans, describing their feelings about the stoves:

"It heats well, uses less firewood, and there is no more smoke in the kitchen."

—Olga Lidia Chicas, family of five, Atlantida, Honduras

"I suffer from asthma, but since I have had the improved stove, my health has improved."

—Reina Jacinta Hernandez, family of six, Copán, Honduras

"For me, the project has been a great benefit since it saves firewood. I had always hoped to have an improved cookstove."

—Jose Santos Sanchez, family of eleven, Francisco Morazán, Honduras

"Less firewood is used with the new stove. Before, I used a lot of firewood in a short time."

—Maria Elsy Benitez, family of five, Intibuca, Honduras

"Your life improves because the stove was made inside the home. The old stove was out in the rain."

—Mayra Elizabeth Fernandez Leiva, family of six, Santa Bárbara, Honduras

"The stove is very good. In an hour I cook six times the food so that they can go to work [in the morning]."

—Leaybin Colindres Cerresto, family of four, El Paraiso, Honduras

"I am delighted with my stove and I have never had such a beautiful thing as this. Thank you."

—Ana Maria Salgado Escobar, family of four, Yoro, Honduras

The road ahead

We traveled everywhere in pickup trucks, with four, six, or even eight of us piled in the back, all positioned to reflect seniority within Mirador. I loved it back there—the fresh air, the views of the countryside, the shared sense of purpose, the comradery.

In the early days, we often talked and debated the design of the stove, its components, and our construction methods. We were all focused on making an effective and affordable stove. As time passed and the multiple benefits of the stove became apparent, our conversations in the back of the pickup truck naturally moved toward growth. We all wanted to build more stoves for more people.

But first...

These conversations about the future were exciting, but also gave me pause. Thinking about future possibilities pulled me back to the necessities of the present. Our stove still needed improvements. Our construction methods were still evolving. We would need to expand staff and training. Our suppliers would need to step up. Was Mirador prepared to grow at scale? More funding would be required. How could we afford to meet the demand?

"Stoves Make You Old"

"In the early 2000s, Richard Lawrence invited me to Honduras to look at the Mirador stove, to help identify any weaknesses in design, and to look for improvements that could be made. I understood Mirador's objectives, for I had been involved in cookstove design and testing for over two decades.

"We spent several days visiting homes in remote hillside villages, inspecting stoves, and speaking with the homeowners. These women use the stove daily and are the ultimate stove experts. Late one afternoon, Richard and I sat on the stoop in front of the last home we would visit that day, processing everything we had learned. Both of us were hot, dusty, and tired. Richard often reminds me of the comment I made at that moment: 'Stoves make you old.'"

—Dean Still, Director of Aprovecho Research Center
and friend of Mirador

FOR ALL WE had accomplished in our first few years, I also understood that we were still a young organization, feeling our way forward. To achieve our hopes for the future, we needed to take stock.

When we did, we found failures in both the stove and within Mirador.

Failures of the stove

We had reached the stage where the earliest stoves were beginning to show weaknesses due to extended use. We needed to turn our focus to strengthening the stove. Like any business, we needed a great product.

If our stove didn't work well for the women who used it, they would stop using it and return to the traditional, inefficient *fogón* and the chronic respiratory ailments it causes. This stove problem was existential. Flawed stove, game over.

We found that every stove component needed to be strengthened, reengineered, or redesigned. Any weakness in the stove, used for seven hours a day, every day of the year, will eventually be exposed.

Dean Still was right: stoves would make us old if we didn't get this right. We got to work.

Durability

The steel *plancha*, the cooking surface of the stove, was often failing. The *plancha* is constantly exposed to direct flame and high heat; even steel will eventually break down under those conditions. Professor Elder devised a solution. He reinforced the bottom of the *plancha* by adding two steel plates, one on each end, right where the flame hits the bottom of the *plancha* above the firebox. When one patch wore out, the cook could turn the *plancha* 180 degrees and extend the life of the *plancha*.

Efficiency

We invited Dean Still to Honduras. He helped us redesign the square *plancha* into a rectangular *plancha*, making the stove more efficient while maintaining the large surface area required for Honduran cooking.

Dee's Corner

The corners of the stove, as originally engineered, cracked repeatedly. My wife, Dee, focused on this and led a redesign in the brick assembly. It was an inexpensive and easy fix, but an example of how even the most minor details needed to change.

Combustion

For more efficient combustion, we added a *parrilla*, the grate upon which the wood is burned, to allow air to pass above and below the wood. This was another low-cost solution that made a huge difference. We should have recognized this earlier.

Supply chain

Our suppliers had to build better ceramic parts and better chimneys. We worked directly with each supplier to improve quality and help them to become more efficient.

Failures at Mirador

We knew that we also had to improve Mirador's operations. We needed to improve staff training, streamline communication with suppliers and homeowners, and become more proactive in every way. We all worked together on these changes.

Also, if we were to build more stoves, we had to improve our efficiency. For this, I had a plan. Not a plan devised by the group, but my plan. The project was called El Molde. Quoting Robert Burns, "The best-laid plans of mice and men often go awry."

El Molde

Everything we do at Mirador is a team effort. We share successes, and we share failures. There is no finger-pointing. But for the following blunder, well-intentioned though it may have been, one can join my colleagues in a good laugh and point a finger of blame directly at me.

I aimed to manufacture the stoves instead of building them on location one at a time in each rural home. My vision was for Mirador to run a factory modeled on the hyper-efficient factories I had visited in Guangdong Province, China. My strategy was to increase production, standardize quality, and drive the cost of the stove down. Scratching out back-of-the-envelope calculations, I foresaw the cost of the stove dropping from $35 to $33, maybe even $29!

I explained my ideas to our competent COO, Professor Elder. Ever my loyal colleague, he agreed to give it a try. Looking back, I am sure he knew right from the start that this would fail.

The Mirador team created a "lab" in an abandoned house on the outskirts of Atima. There we designed a mold (El Molde) for each part of the stove structure. We figured out how to interlock all the pieces. My colleagues built the molds perfectly to the design, poured cement, and put the stove together.

My idea immediately began to show cracks: cracks in the strategy and cracks in the stoves. Building the stoves with the molds took too much time, and the stoves were too heavy and fragile to transport on the mountain roads. But as the Hondurans know, I am stubborn. We pushed on.

Eventually, Professor Elder had to quietly pull my wife Dee aside to ask her to please convince me to stop the El Molde project. "Stop?" I asked, "Why?" Well, it was shown that our Honduran technicians, skilled and hardworking, could build a better stove faster and more cheaply than El Molde ever would. I had to surrender.

Ultimately, El Molde, disaster though it was, taught me a good lesson. We didn't need a cheaper stove; we needed a better stove. We needed to focus on the basics, to invest in training, simple technology, communication, stronger parts, a more effective stove design, a more durable stove, and nearly every other part of the Mirador program.

The lessons learned by El Molde allowed us to face our next great challenge.

This photograph shows the Mirador team celebrating our first completed
El Molde stove. My colleagues were only smiling out of respect for me.

El Cinco

"¿Por qué dejaste de
usar la estufa?"

"Why did you stop
using the stove?"

"No se calienta!"

"It doesn't get hot!"

The holy grail of stove projects

THE MOST ACCURATE predictor of a low-quality stove project is a high year-one abandonment rate, or the percentage of stoves that fall out of use within 12 months after construction. A low abandonment rate, on the other hand, is the holy grail for any stove project.

If the stove does not work well, homeowners will stop using it. And if that should happen, rebuilding confidence is nearly impossible. There are few second chances in the stove business.

There are many examples of failed stove projects around the world. Predictably, almost all of them suffer from high year-one abandonment rates.

In our early years, Mirador had no hard data on our abandonment rate, but on our trips, we allocated time to review stoves built six or 12 months earlier. The numbers were not good.

I wanted nothing to do with failure. We had to figure this out. We did not know why the stoves were being abandoned, and I certainly did not

41

have the solution. But I did have my partner, Professor Elder Mendoza, a master problem solver.

El Cinco

In October 2022, we gathered in a ballroom in San Pedro Sula, the industrial heart of Honduras, to celebrate the construction of 285,000 stoves. Our hometown of Santa Bárbara had no facility to accommodate the 120 of our 250 employees who attended, so we held the event in San Pedro Sula. At dinner, I gave a speech describing the story of how Professor Elder solved our abandonment rate problem:

> Most of you will not remember the early years of Mirador. But there were many problems, dark days, and lots of challenges.
>
> I want to tell you about one specific day I spent in San Pedrito, a town just outside of Atima. It was one of the most critical moments in the life of Proyecto Mirador.
>
> The Mirador team was in San Pedrito to check stoves that were six or 12 months old. As we went from one house to another, we found abandoned stoves and ladies who told us the stove didn't work.

"¿Por qué dejaste de usar la estufa?"	*"Why did you stop using the stove?"*
"¡No se calienta!"	*"It doesn't get hot!"*
"¿Por qué no se calienta?"	*"Why doesn't it get hot?"*
"No sé, señor. Simplemente no se calienta."	*"I don't know, sir. It just doesn't get hot."*

At that time, I thought the problem was with the ladies somehow misusing the stove. But actually, the problem turned out to be the level of the wood ash under the *plancha* (the cooktop). If the ash level got too high, it would block the draft and suffocate the fire. If the ash level got too low, the draft would not start. I understood that until we could secure a consistent level of ash one inch below the *plancha*, Mirador's stove simply could not succeed.

This was more than discouraging; it was maddening! Was it possible that wood ash was going to derail our stove and become a Valley of Death for Mirador?

At the end of that frustrating afternoon, as we walked along a dirt path in San Pedrito, lost in thought, a herd of about 30 cows ran toward us and separated Professor Elder and me to the sides of the path. When the cows passed, Professor Elder rejoined me and said, "I have an idea."

Soon after, Professor Elder sent me some photos of his solution: a simple steel bar, 18 inches long and one inch wide. It functioned like a windshield wiper to maintain the ash at the optimal height. It worked perfectly. This one-dollar piece of metal had saved Mirador.

Professor Elder's solution came to be called El Cinco, meaning "five" in Spanish. Designed primarily to help the homeowner maintain the correct level of wood ash, it also allows them to carry out all five simple but necessary stove maintenance steps. As El Cinco was incorporated into our stove operations in the following months, our abandonment rate began to plummet to levels not seen in any other stove project in the Americas.

Professor Elder Mendoza demonstrates how to use the *Cinco* maintenance tool to maintain the proper level of ash under the cooktop.

El Dos por Tres

"Kids say the darndest things."

—Art Linkletter

So much had changed!

By 2008, we had redesigned and improved nearly every aspect of the stove. But we realized that La Justa, a generic name for a broad classification of stoves with "rocket" combustion chambers, no longer accurately described the upgraded Mirador stove. We needed to give our stove a new name that might speak to its uniqueness.

To address this, we decided to run a stove-naming contest in one of the remote communities where we had built our stove in recent months. We asked the local students to suggest a name, paint a picture of the stove, and state its utility. At that time, the schoolteachers were out on strike since the government had not paid their salaries. But the community became so enthused that the teachers agreed to return to the school to help manage the contest.

We soon received about 40 submissions. We delighted in giving out prizes to the winners of the best painting and the best description of the stove. But the real winner was Reina Jaquelin Mejia, a young elementary student from the village La Vega in San Francisco de Ojuera, who wrote a small, modest "2x3" in the upper corner of her painting. The name struck the Hondurans in a snap of the fingers.

45

In Honduras, 2x3, or *dos por tres*, is a common phrase for doing something quickly, "in an instant." It fits our stove perfectly. In an instant, we get the smoke out of the house. In an instant, we build the stove. It heats up *en un dos por tres*. The name caught on immediately. Today nearly every rural Honduran knows the name Dos por Tres.

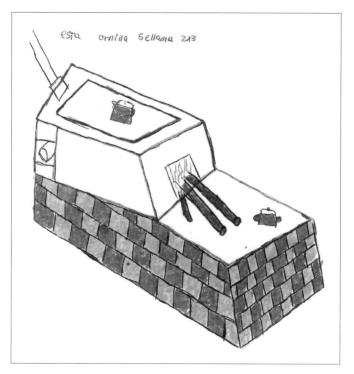

The winning submission from Reina Jaquelin Mejia, who named the Dos por Tres (see 2x3 in small letters at top).

Word gets around

Having fixed many of the weaknesses of the stove with better materials, and with Professor Elder's breakthrough invention of El Cinco, solicitations for the Dos por Tres began to flood into our office from communities across Honduras.

The solicitations were simply a reflection of the success of the stove with

Honduran women. The cooks loved our stove, and by word-of-mouth, their neighbors, cousins, and friends all wanted one. Honduran women were making their voices heard. It was social media without a single computer or mobile phone. We received stacks of paper solicitations for the Dos por Tres that mayors, relatives, and homeowners delivered personally to our offices.

We didn't spend a dollar on marketing. We didn't need to—word-of-mouth did it all—and the money was better spent building more stoves. And today, 19 years later, we still do not spend money on marketing. The stove speaks for itself, as do the people who use it. This is the best and most gratifying testimony to the utility of our stove.

A stack of solicitations for Dos por Tres stoves.

Party crasher

Back in 2004, Cielo had called on family members and friends to fund the first 29 stoves, but even with their continued generosity, we could only fund some of the stoves that Hondurans needed and wanted. I had a day job and did not have the time to raise funds in a significant way.

Yet as solicitations poured in, we felt a profound responsibility to provide our solution to the thousands of Honduran homes that got so little support from the government.

And now, with the stove improved and all those new solicitations coming in, funding had become our primary barrier to scale and success. Would this become another Valley of Death moment for Mirador? How could we solve this?

The journey toward a long-term funding solution would begin in the small, remote village of Valle de la Cruz in the hills of Western Honduras. That story is told in the next chapter.

Deforestation

"Anything else you are interested in is not going to happen if you cannot breathe the air and drink the water. Don't sit this one out. Do something."

—Carl Sagan

I N THE LATE afternoon sun in Valle de la Cruz, a village near Atima, we sat on the wide front stoop of a bodega. We had been building stoves all day, and Elder brought out an armful of cold Coca-Colas to our exhausted and thirsty group of gringos and Hondurans. Tim Longwell was also with us. Tim was a forestry professor at Colorado State University, temporarily teaching at Zamorano University, the prominent agricultural university in Central America. We had invited Tim to join us for a few days to learn about our work.

Across the dusty dirt road before us was a soccer field where some local kids played a pickup game. Beyond the soccer field, in the near distance, was a large, steep hill, almost triangular in shape, and only sparsely dotted with trees.

Seeing is understanding

Gesturing toward the hill, I asked Tim if he could explain for us the phenomenon of deforestation. He looked at the hill for a few moments, nodded, and then, in excellent Spanish, began to speak.

He described in clear layperson's terms the effects of soil erosion, the destruction of wildlife habitat, the lack of water retention, and the inevitable decline in biodiversity. None of us spoke, listening and looking as Tim pointed out that the remaining trees on the hillside were modest in size, growing in thin patches. "All the biggest trees have been cut down. The healthy trees won't come back. All that's left are the genetically weaker trees that will never reach the strength of their ancestors."

The Hondurans shifted uncomfortably on the stoop. For the first time in their lives, they understood academically what they knew instinctively: their forests were degrading. We all sat quietly, staring at the hill. The largest trees had been harvested by timber companies owned by wealthy Honduran families who never replanted a single tree. But cutting wood to fuel inefficient cookstoves was also a significant part of the problem. And now, we realized our stoves would be a part of the solution if we could continue building enough of them.

Deforestation, typical for rural Honduras.

The next day we awoke with a new sense of urgency. The Mirador team's aspirations were bigger. Our determination was stronger. We had to remain dogged in improving our stove, scaling our operations, and sourcing new ways to finance our growth. Our perseverance would help us achieve our aspirations.

Part of something bigger

I realized that the sad image of that degraded hillside in Valle de la Cruz was only part of the picture. I knew from our research that 400,000 homes were using old inefficient cookstoves in Honduras alone and as many as 800 million homes worldwide. This was a global problem. There was a small cohort of other improved cookstove projects in the Global South, but we would need thousands more.

Persistence and aspiration had become part of our culture at Mirador and would become a core part of our business model. Now, we needed that same persistence and aspiration on a global scale. That is easier said than done. What could elevate the importance of this work in the public mind? How could this possibly be funded?

An environmentalist in Boston, whom you will meet in the next chapter, would soon open my eyes to the answer to that question.

PART TWO

Funding Mirador

Climate Change Changed Everything

"Climate change is real. The science is compelling. And the longer we wait, the harder the problem will be to solve."

—John F. Kerry, United States Special Presidential Envoy for Climate

W E MEET COUNTLESS people throughout our lives, many of whom bring us joy and enrich us. But now and then, we meet a special person at just the right time, when interests align and whole new horizons open.

Jeremy Grantham

I had the good fortune to be introduced by a mutual business client to Jeremy Grantham, founder of GMO, the successful fund management company, and founder of The Grantham Foundation for the Protection of the Environment. I first met Jeremy when I was in Boston to meet clients. He must have thought I was a bit overdressed in my suit and tie, as he was expecting to see a stove project developer rather than an investor. We talked about Proyecto Mirador's work building stoves in rural Honduras and his interest in the environment. We promised to meet again.

My business takes me to Boston at least twice yearly, and Jeremy was always gracious enough to meet with me. We got on well, and over time, a friendship developed. Jeremy would always ask about our work at Mirador and soon generously supported Mirador by donating $10,000 to our cause. As we did for all our donors, we sent Jeremy reports on our work in Honduras, dedicated stoves in his honor, and updated him with both our successes and failures.

On one memorable visit, I caught Jeremy on an uncharacteristically slow day and we lingered in his office overlooking Boston Harbor. We discussed our common interests: investing, China, managing clients, and the difficulty of stock picking. I remember he spoke insightfully that day of a looming commodity shortage. As the noon hour approached, I asked if I was taking too much of his time. Jeremy replied, "Would you join me for lunch?"

An unforgettable lunch

We walked down the street to Legal Seafood. When the waiter asked us if we would like something to drink, I waited for Jeremy to decide whether he would have water or iced tea. To my surprise, he told the waiter he would like "a glass of the cheapest white wine on your list." "Make that two," I said. I still sometimes use Jeremy's line to order the cheapest wine on a restaurant's list, much to my pleasure and my wife's horrified embarrassment.

It was a great lunch. Jeremy shared stories of his experiences serving on the boards of many of the leading environmental non-profits, and then the conversation naturally turned to the subject of climate change. Although Jeremy usually speaks in a quiet and affable manner, his tone and urgency changed when he spoke about climate change that day. He expressed alarm about the trajectory of global emissions and deep concern over how climate change would impact the financial markets. His frustration with the world's slow progress was palpable.

This conversation occurred when the reality of climate change was still dawning and still being debated. With factual clarity, Jeremy cut through the complexity and confusion. His expertise on the subject was unmatched. I admired his passion, his commitment, and his entrepreneurial perspective. I had so much to learn. Jeremy made me understand that fighting climate change was an urgent moral imperative for us all.

History will show that Jeremy was the first voice in the finance industry to raise the red flag over climate change, and our meetings became the highlight of my semi-annual trips to Boston.

Practical activism

In his fight against climate change, Jeremy was determined and fearless. He mentioned to me on one visit that he was headed to Washington, DC, that very weekend, to join a protest at the White House for more action on climate change. He added that he might even chain himself to the White House fence. No one in my close experience had ever shown such a high-minded commitment to an issue since my mother marched for women's rights in DC in the 1960s.

Thankfully, in the end, Jeremy didn't need to chain himself to the fence to express his passion. Jeremy, in his wisdom, focuses his activism on practical and effective actions. Eventually, I realized he is the foremost entrepreneurial philanthropist leading the fight against climate change. *Entrepreneurial philanthropist.* This concept was new to me then, and Jeremy's example has inspired me ever since. It is an ideal to which the wealthy should aspire.

A pivotal book

In one of our discussions, Jeremy gave me another piece of invaluable advice: he suggested I read *The Economics of Climate Change* by Lord Nicholas Stern.

This book was published in 2006, and I was intrigued by its discussion of the economic aspect of climate change. With a degree in economics, I was naturally fascinated that climate change was not just pure science.

It became one of the most important books of my life.

The in-depth research of Lord Stern and his team from Cambridge left no room for doubt: the world was releasing too much CO_2 into the atmosphere, and the planet was undergoing frightening changes. The book was filled with powerful examples from around the globe that painted a vivid picture of what was to come, including:

- The Nile River in Egypt, by some projections, could lose 75% of its water flow by the end of this century, with all of the bleak environmental, humanitarian, and geopolitical ramifications that would entail.

- Mass migration could drive hundreds of millions of people away from their homes to survive resource scarcity, desertification, droughts, floods, and rising sea levels. Honduras, and much of Central America, is already a living example of people migrating north to escape destructive hurricanes and repeated droughts.

- Larger, more destructive storms will continue to occur and with greater frequency. The catastrophic hurricanes that have occurred in recent years are but a prologue of what could come.

Importantly, Lord Stern also told us that if we start early, the cost of climate change is comparatively modest. If we start later, the costs are exponentially higher. I realized that the world would behave like an 18-year-old student, procrastinating until the very last moment to cram for an all-important exam.

The scope of the problem

Lord Stern's book drove me to research climate change further on my own, including the annual presentation by Professor John Holdren of Harvard which documents the latest science on all aspects of climate change. I also recall an eye-opening article from *Rolling Stone* in 2013, "Miami: How Rising Sea Levels Threaten South Florida," which described the ignored and seemingly insurmountable problem of Miami's geology. There was a lot to learn, more than I could have anticipated. You may know many of these stories by now:

- Glacier melting in Greenland and Antarctica poses an imminent threat to the entire globe as sea levels continue to rise.

- Unchecked leaks from the oil and gas industry, landfills, and agriculture result in the release of methane, a greenhouse gas 84 times more potent than CO_2.

- Disrupted migratory patterns and habitat loss have put 389 North American bird species at risk of extinction.

- Benzene, a cancer-causing compound, is known to leak from gas stoves in the home, even when they are turned off.

The list goes on… and on… and on. It is the scope of the problem that leaves us all feeling helpless.

What can we do as individuals? When we look for answers, we discover that the simple act of reducing emissions in our own lives is complicated and frustrating.

But there was an answer to that question, at least a partial answer.

A role for Mirador?

As I learned more and more about climate change, the many lessons from Lord Stern's book stayed fresh in my mind. One lesson became particularly relevant: any action to reduce carbon emissions was worthwhile. I returned to that section of the book to see my old notes penciled in the margin: Mirador? Dos por Tres?

I explained the simple thought process to my colleagues at Mirador:

- Climate change is real.

- The world needs to reduce CO_2 emissions.

- Our stove could reduce carbon emissions at a low cost.

- Wouldn't building more stoves be a good thing for the planet?

We all agreed that more stoves were needed urgently, but the same perennial question arose to haunt us once again: How could we fund the growth that so many people, and now even our planet, needed so desperately?

A breakthrough at the MIT Bookstore

In 2007, after one of my meetings with Jeremy, I was searching for more information on climate change. I wandered into the MIT Bookstore in Cambridge and walked directly to the Environment section. The best books on the subject should be here. My eye caught a bright blue, yellow, and black cover. The book was entitled *Voluntary Carbon Markets*, written by Ricardo Bayon and others.

I had not been looking for a book specifically on carbon markets, but I was immediately interested after picking it up and reading about a mechanism that could put a price on carbon. In my earlier reading of *The Economics of Climate Change*, Lord Stern taught me that putting a price on emitting carbon would be essential to incentivize humans to reduce emissions. And if emitting carbon has a cost, reducing carbon emissions should have commensurate value. Could Voluntary Carbon Markets make that connection in the real world?

I bought the book. It gave me an excellent introduction to the workings of the Voluntary Carbon Markets (VCM) and Gold Standard certification. It illuminated the potential for those who reduce carbon emissions to quantify those reduced emissions and sell them as carbon credits to individuals or companies who wish to offset their emissions. That's the power of the VCM: to give carbon reductions true economic value. In the VCM, the fight against climate change might have a viable economic framework.

I read the book with unusual intensity. I was introduced to all sorts of new concepts: standards, methodologies, offset project types, project verifiers, offset credit retailers, and institutional buyers. I didn't know these terminologies, but institutional buyers especially caught my attention. Capital! Here it was: Mirador could sell carbon credits for cash!

Carbon reductions must be verifiable to have any real value as carbon credits, and several independent verification Standards, or programs, perform such work. Still, the Gold Standard was the only Standard with a cookstove methodology at that time. The authors cautioned that the verification methodology was tough. OK, I didn't know what that meant, but I have had auditors review and certify financial statements for many years. How strict could the Gold Standard be? And the concept of carbon finance was the only viable solution I had found to solve Mirador's funding challenge.

Two interrelated issues, one possible solution

Ricardo Bayon and his co-authors focused my mind on two issues that needed to be addressed:

- First, rural homes in Honduras and across the developing world needed clean-burning, low-emission stoves.

- Second, to address climate change, the world needed to reduce the emissions of CO_2 into the atmosphere.

The two problems are interrelated: carbon projects are the ultimate local problem, and climate change is the ultimate global problem. When taken together, local carbon reduction projects, like Mirador, have global reach and can contribute to the fight against climate change.

Could the Gold Standard help Mirador, and so many other impactful projects around the world, mobilize capital in exchange for their contributions to climate change mitigation? Would companies and individuals buy carbon credits? In their efforts to combat climate change, would institutional buyers also be willing to value the health, economic, and social benefits to the rural poor that are fundamental to Global South projects?

We were skeptical, but the scale of our financing problem in Honduras was so severe that we had no other reasonable alternative. Without financing, Mirador was still facing that Valley of Death.

Upon my return to California, I told Esther Adams, my assistant of many years, "Esther, we need to sell carbon credits. Mirador needs to get Gold Standard certified."

She just stared at me.

Gold Standard Certification

"Gold Standard made Mirador a better project."

—Richard H. Lawrence, Jr.

FUNDING WAS OUR albatross. It was holding us back. As I had learned in my reading, carbon credits could possibly solve that.

However, for Mirador's carbon credits to have real value, our carbon reductions had to be verified. It seemed apparent that our stoves saved wood and that our stove was superior in every way to the traditional *fogón*. Wasn't it enough for Mirador to simply state that? No. We needed proof. We needed third-party confirmation of scientifically verified data to substantiate our emission reduction claims.

The Gold Standard had the only certification scheme with a cookstove methodology at that time. We expected that Gold Standard Certification would be rigorous, which we appreciated. Rigorous verification is necessary to confirm a project's credibility for buyers of credits. So, in 2007, we set out to become Gold Standard certified.

Really, how tough could it be?

As a stock picker and investment manager by profession, I was accustomed to the rigorous process of auditing a company's financial accounts. Gold Standard certification made that seem like a cakewalk. Gold Standard project certification was more akin to creating a full-blown, SEC-approved prospectus for an initial public offering of shares—and repeating it every year.

Although at times we became annoyed at the tedious requirements, we understood that Gold Standard Certification was a market-based solution and offered us the best way to connect fuel-efficient stoves in rural Honduras with North American capital. There was no other viable way to achieve that. The Gold Standard would take time, but it provided us an opportunity to transform Mirador from an informal effort into a self-funding stove project. If successful, it would provide a financing solution for the long term.

Gold Standard requires two key steps for issuing a project's carbon credits: Certification and Verification. Bear with us, as readers must understand the detailed requirements to sell carbon credits.

Phase One: Gold Standard Certification

In simplified terms, Certification is the process by which the project, both the physical stove and the Mirador organization, is confirmed to conform with the Gold Standard methodology. Sounds easy. It is not.

We needed to prove arcane concepts such as additionality, leakage, abandonment rate, degradation in the performance of the stove, and perhaps the most complex and difficult, fNRB (fraction of non-renewable biomass), which denotes the percentage of forest cover in the project area that is determined to be non-renewable.

My assistant, Esther Adams, always competent and professional, was with me in the trenches of our Gold Standard effort. She tells this story:

I came to work for Richard Lawrence in April 2006. I had always enjoyed taking on new challenges and considered myself unusually adaptable and good at figuring stuff out.

So, when Richard came into my office in 2007, briefly explained the concept of carbon credits, told me we would need to submit a Gold Standard Project Design Document, and handed me an early draft, I cheerfully accepted the challenge.

Forty pages and six scientific equations later, I had to admit defeat. More than any other project I had ever approached, this was squarely out of my league. I made a few proofreading marks to avoid looking completely stupid and sent it back to Richard. His answer? Not so fast. With more than a bit of trepidation, I set about trying, as best I could, to understand the task before me.

Thus began the mother of all checklists.

We also needed a lot of outside assistance to meet the challenge, including cookstove experts, forest scientists, carbon accounting experts, thermal engineers specialized in cookstoves (whom I fondly refer to as stove tinkerers), grad students, and field workers. A partial list includes:

- Erik Wurster and Evan Haigler of UpEnergy and Impact Carbon, who had developed the world's first three Gold Standard registered cookstove projects, helped us become the fourth.

- Dean Still and Nordica McCarty at Aprovecho Research Institute, leading cookstove scientists, assisted throughout in proving our stove saved carbon.

- Rob Bailis, PhD, formerly of the Yale School of Forestry & Environmental Studies, introduced us to the Kitchen Performance Test to quantify stove performance and use in the field, and to measure the degradation in performance over time. He also performed the research that enabled us to determine the elusive fNRB value described above.

We pressed on. Step by step, we slowly worked our way through the process. A third-party auditor, then called a UN DOE (United Nations

Designated Operational Entity), visited our headquarters in Honduras and toured the project. Two representatives of the Gold Standard, Ivan Hernandez and Lisa Rosen, also visited Mirador. Finally, on June 29, 2010, three years after we had begun the process, we became the world's fourth certified Gold Standard cookstove project.

Reaching Gold Standard Certification was only the beginning. We still had to pass more scrutiny in order to get the credits. A barrage of on-site tests and studies would be needed.

Phase Two: Gold Standard Verification

By the end of 2010, Mirador had built over 12,000 stoves since inception, with plans to build almost that many again in 2011 alone. We also had to charge ahead with Gold Standard Verification, Step Two of this process.

Verification is the process by which a project is confirmed by Gold Standard to have been implemented as certified, with monitoring systems in place, and with carbon emissions unequivocally proven. As with Certification, this also sounds easy enough. Also, it was not.

Kitchen Performance Tests, for example, were carried out in Honduran homes over four full days, measuring actual fuelwood consumption during normal day-to-day cooking activities. Baseline data were then compared against project data to determine how much Mirador's Dos por Tres stove reduced fuelwood use.

Then, another elaborate study was required to determine fNRB, involving aerial surveys using remote sensing with lidar technology, with the loss of forest cover evaluated over time through GIS technology.

Everything we did had to be meticulously documented. We suffered through rounds and rounds of reviews. We learned about CARs (Corrective Action Requests), CLs (Clarification Requests), and FARs (Forward Action Requests).

We had started out thinking this was as simple as the financial audits I had been through, but it was not.

We felt insulted, frustrated, and at times, unfairly treated. We were so challenged and criticized that we felt beaten down. But each time a new question arose, Doña Emilia and Professor Elder, along with all the Mirador team in Honduras, always had the answer. They were almost preternaturally well organized. And eventually, despite the difficulties we faced, progress was made, and we began to realize that the Gold Standard was undeniably making us a better project.

Success at last

Finally, Mirador's first Gold Standard Verification was confirmed. On April 7, 2011, over four years since I arrived back at my California office and told Esther we were going to sell carbon credits, the first 12,368 carbon credits were formally issued to Proyecto Mirador. The credits were sold to a German coffee company at $20 per tonne, for a grand total of $247,360.

Exhausted but happy, we opened the champagne, our indignation now tempered with gratitude and humility. We did not know at the time that we would not see a $20/tonne price again. Indeed, the carbon market was headed into a protracted bear market, and eventually, we hit a punishing low of $3.25 per tonne. In 2023, at the time of writing, we have yet to reach our initial high. But in 2011 we didn't care about what the bear market would bring. It was a day of great celebration in Honduras and San Francisco after four years of heavy lifting. With full Gold Standard accreditation, we had a capital source for the long term. Mirador could grow as hoped.

A month or so later, my wife and I, while in Europe for other meetings, traveled to Germany to meet the buyer. We were looking forward to showing off our proud baby, Proyecto Mirador. They canceled the meeting at the last minute. That confused us. Odd... ominous... concerning; perhaps it was a sign that the bear market was about to unfold. Since we had non-refundable tickets, we also learned Hamburg was a dull city in the winter.

Capital to grow Mirador

In September 2010, as we were advancing through our first Gold Standard Verification, Jeremy Grantham, through the Grantham Foundation for the Protection of the Environment, joined the Lawrence family to capitalize Proyecto Mirador with donated equity. Jeremy's support and that of his wife, Hanne, legitimized Proyecto Mirador and validated our efforts at overcoming obstacles over six years in Honduras.

In the Granthams' view, Proyecto Mirador presented a win-win-win: time saved from collecting less firewood, health benefits from reduced indoor air pollution, and reduced forest degradation. These were the critical factors that drove the Grantham Foundation to support Mirador. In September 2010, Jeremy and I transferred our respective commitments into the Proyecto Mirador account, and we finally breathed a sigh of relief.

Gold Standard Certification made Mirador a better project, verified our carbon reductions, and allowed us to sell carbon credits. That, along with the donated capital from the Grantham Foundation and the Lawrence family, gave us the financial footing to pursue our long-term goals. Another major piece of the Mirador model had been achieved.

The task before us now was to grow Mirador and perform at a high level. Thankfully, my partners in Honduras were up to the challenge.

The paper legacy of Mirador's Gold Standard Certification
and first Verification.

The Mirador Project
Was Also Faulty

"An abandoned stove is no good to anyone."

—Juan Carlos Guzmán, Leader of Team Ghostbusters,
Proyecto Mirador

WE HAD FIXED our stove, renamed it the Dos por Tres, and identified a revenue stream through Gold Standard certification and sales of carbon credits. Demand for the stove from rural communities continued to surge. We were flat-out busy.

Managing a growing business

It was great that our stoves were in high demand, but Mirador itself needed to be operationally effective in handling the growth we had created. We needed to manage our development and not let growth manage us. Mirador had grown into a complex business and needed to be managed professionally. We realized that Mirador's growth had exposed faults that had to be addressed if we were to become the organization we envisioned. We prioritized critical parts of our program for improvement and focused our efforts accordingly.

By early 2010, we had a two-year backlog of requests for stoves from homeowners. To accelerate the pace of installations, we decided to transfer a portion of the responsibility for stove construction to local microenterprises that employed local labor to build stoves for Mirador. We called the leaders of these microenterprises *Ejecutores*. We invested in a training program for the *Ejecutores* and their technicians, including a training center for building stoves. It also included a communications program that taught technicians how to instruct homeowners effectively on the use and maintenance of the stove. This program was a huge success for local communities and Mirador.

In 2011 we hired a team of supervisors whose job was to return to the homes three times after installation at specific intervals to ensure that stove maintenance was done correctly, thus maximizing successful adoption of the stove and minimizing costly year-one abandonment rates. This was a first in the global cookstove business.

In 2012 we upgraded the facilities of our suppliers. We installed fuel-efficient kilns for the ceramic makers and modern steel-cutting equipment in the *plancha* factory, among other improvements.

In 2014 we built *Edificio Giron*, an office for Mirador administration, which included a warehouse to store ever-larger inventory and a training center for employees. We created a wall in the office to display all the events of Mirador's history, to document for our employees and visitors the many successes we had enjoyed, as well as the challenges we had faced and overcome. It was essential for all employees to understand why we build great stoves.

We worked to improve communications with the homeowners by circulating a comprehensive Use and Maintenance Brochure and conveying information through a structured program of community meetings and one-on-one training. The women in rural communities needed to understand our objectives as a non-profit.

In 2014, we expanded our team of supervisors to increase follow-up visits and thus ensure proper use and care of the stove. It was a time of growth and energy.

Proud owner of a new Dos por Tres holding the Use and Maintenance Brochure.

Ghostbusters

Gradually we became aware that there were certain stoves that, despite being appropriately built, simply did not heat up. We determined that gremlins—or *duendes*, in Spanish—must be living in these stoves, causing them to malfunction. We established a group of stove experts and engineers that we called Team Ghostbusters, whose job was to roam around rural communities, identify problems with the stove, and kill the *duendes*.

With their insights and solutions, the Ghostbusters identified previously unpredictable weaknesses in the stove where the *duendes* were causing problems. We implemented more valuable improvements in the stove's operation, placement, and design.

The story is well told by Juan Carlos Guzmán, the leader of Team Ghostbusters, who has been with Mirador for many years.

> Our team, along with Richard Lawrence and a group of stove experts, visited homes in the village of Las Alejandras Taulabe to check for potential issues that could be affecting performance in the Dos por Tres stoves. There, we decided to create a team of Maintenance Specialists, which we named Team Ghostbusters. Our job was to kill the *duendes*.
>
> We visited homes where supervisors in the field had reported problems. One common issue we confronted was that certain stoves did not heat well, a situation that had pestered us for years. We finally discovered that it was caused by the tops of chimneys being lower than the peak of the house or blocked by tree branches. In all our years of building stoves, we never anticipated the chimney height could cause the stove not to heat up. For less obvious problems, we began to use the equipment for measuring heat and airflow. We employed a thermal camera to collect statistical data that would allow us to detect the existence of the *duendes* and identify an effective solution.
>
> With time and practice, whatever the problem, we would find the cause, kill the *duende*, and get the stove back in operation. An abandoned stove is no good to anyone.

Our next challenge

These improvements to Mirador's systems were significant, but one last challenge still lay ahead. We needed to automate our operations.

"*Mejor Que Nunca!*"

"I didn't know anything about computers back then. I had never even turned one on!"

—Fredy Pineda, *Ejecutor*, Proyecto Mirador, 2011

I N T H E P R E V I O U S chapter, we described how professionalizing Mirador was necessary if we were to continue to grow. But our work was not done yet.

Until now, Mirador had been a paper place, with information manually recorded and stored in filing cabinets. By 2010, we were maxed out under that old system, stuck in the past, with the future out of reach. There was no choice: Mirador needed to be automated. But this story is not just about technology. It is a story about the people who made it work.

Out with the old...

Reniery Rodriguez, Mirador's IT Manager, describes Mirador's old paper systems:

> In the early days of Proyecto Mirador, stove installations were tracked on pre-printed forms with location and homeowner information. At the end of each month, supervisors delivered the paperwork to the Mirador office in Santa Bárbara to be organized and forwarded to our office in California, where it was processed

and analyzed. This system worked well enough in the early years; in the first seven years that we had been building stoves, from 2004 through 2010, Mirador had built a total of about 12,000 stoves. But now, by 2011, we would build that many stoves in a single year. We needed a better system to be able to do that.

...In with the new

Automating Mirador's systems was bound to be a complex task, involving not only new software, hardware, and new procedures, but also because none of Mirador's staff in Honduras, from Doña Emilia to our newest employee, had ever run anything digitally. A Mirador *Ejecutor*, Fredy Pineda, remembers, "I didn't know anything about computers back then. I had never even turned one on!"

In 2011, the decision was made to hire Stevan Simich of Mogli Technologies to create a data management system for Mirador. We needed hard data, reliably recorded and easily accessible from anywhere. It had to be user-friendly. And at a minimum, the system had to digitally track stove installations, store homeowner information and location, record follow-up visits to verify that stoves were working correctly or to schedule repairs, and contain all the data needed to show carbon reduction statistics for Gold Standard verification.

Expect the unexpected

Stevan Simich and his team worked closely with us to design the system in early 2011. By summer, it was ready for the Mirador team in Honduras. I will let Stevan relate that story:

> In all our tests, the systems worked flawlessly. We were ready to start delivery and training. We configured some rugged Lenovo laptops that operated offline and could be synced later with integrated mobile SIM cards or an internet connection. We even provided protective cases with shoulder straps so supervisors could carry them on their motorcycles.

When we introduced the laptops to the Mirador team in Honduras, however, I saw their initial excitement quickly change to concern. They spoke amongst themselves for a few moments until they finally turned to me and said, "Stevan, these laptops are a dream come true. But if we ride on our motorcycles into a village with this laptop over our shoulder, we may be robbed." Welcome to Honduras: that was a humbling and eye-opening lesson for me.

Fortunately, the system had also been designed to work with iPhones, and when I unveiled a stack of iPhones to the team, their excitement returned. A phone could be carried in a pocket or a backpack and brought out only when needed inside the home. The team liked that all the information about any stove could be recorded immediately on the phone and shared on the cloud. Homeowner information could even be downloaded directly from ID cards.

Implementing Salesforce technology in Honduras: Eugenio Zaldivar and Fredy Pineda, Mirador *Ejecutores*, with their new laptops.

The best maps in Honduras

Mirador's growth over the years had brought us further and further afield into the Honduran countryside, to hundreds of villages and tens of thousands of homes. We were keeping track of all that was essential. Supervisors, for instance, returned to each home where a stove had been installed one, seven, and 13 months after construction.

We wasted a lot of time trying to find all the stoves in the villages. We needed maps. The problem was that there were no good maps of rural Honduras. The available paper maps didn't even show many of the small communities where we worked, and digital maps of Honduras were only available at low resolution.

The solution arose by chance encounter. While picking up his young child at preschool, Stevan Simich reconnected with a friend and fellow parent who worked at Digital Globe, which at that time was launching a new satellite program for custom digital mapping. So, Proyecto Mirador flew satellites over Honduras, and with the result, we had the most accurate maps of Honduras available anywhere. The digital maps were a game changer. On an iPhone, Mirador staff could pinpoint any home within three meters.

Detail of stove installations in Mata de Plátano, Honduras.

"This is our mission."

I expected some speed bumps during the adoption of the new technology. What I did not expect to find—six months later, on my next trip to Honduras—was that most local staff had gone back to the paper system.

I was not happy that we had invested capital into an IT system that wasn't being used. But more than that, I had previously failed to impress upon the Honduran team that IT was necessary if we were to grow. The technology was not a bunch of new-fangled toys: it was essential to Mirador's future. Professor Elder Mendoza, Mirador's COO and inventor of El Cinco, which rescued Mirador from a previous Valley of Death, tells this moving story:

> Many of us were terrified to leave paper behind and embrace technology. But then, Don Ricardo gathered us together one day and told us how important technology was if Mirador was to succeed. That made us think. Mirador has been a school for all, an employment opportunity, and a generator of social and economic development for many families. But the most important accomplishments are the many lives we have saved by removing smoke from homes and our contributions to improving the environment. This is our mission.
>
> We needed technology if we were to fulfill that mission. We learned to use it.

"Mejor que nunca!"

At the beginning of this chapter, Fredy Pineda told us, "I didn't know anything about computers." That was in 2011. In the years since, Fredy and his team have built over 52,000 stoves, managing construction, materials, staffing, logistics, follow-up visits, repairs, and scheduling, all through a digital platform. It is a complex operation, managed well.

A few years ago, I had the opportunity to spend a day with Fredy, driving in his pickup truck to a village where his team was at work. His laptop was open on the seat between us. He navigated by the digital map on his phone to the GPS coordinates from his database. I asked him, "How are you doing, Fredy? How's everything going?"

With a smile, he looked toward me and said, *"Mejor que nunca, Don Ricardo, mejor que nunca!"*

"Better than ever!"

Map showing Mirador stove installations in Honduras and Guatemala in 2022.

The Top of
the Pyramid

"It is one of the projects I'm most proud of."

—Lisa Shibata, Director of Sustainability, Chipotle Mexican Grill,
commenting on Mirador

ALL THE EFFORTS of our previous years had been to transform Mirador from an informal attempt to install stoves into a great carbon project and to push Mirador to the Top of the Pyramid. We had made great strides, we felt.

Still, the true test would come in the carbon market, when everything about Mirador would be scrutinized compared to other carbon projects around the globe, many of which were sponsored by some of the biggest and most widely known environmental groups in climate change mitigation. Our test came when we were introduced to Lisa Shibata.

At that time, Lisa was the senior manager of environment and sustainability at a Fortune 100 company and had led an aggressive program to reduce and offset its greenhouse gas emissions. She was incredibly experienced. She was intelligent. She asked the right questions. She understood what distinguished the best carbon projects. After initial conversations and a review of Mirador's documentation, she agreed to visit our project.

In December 2013, Lisa arrived in Santa Bárbara, Honduras, visiting homes where Dos por Tres stoves were installed, as well as homes still using the traditional *fogón* for comparison. She met with our staff and suppliers, reviewed Mirador's reporting and methodologies, queried our community outreach, and reviewed our maintenance and follow-up procedures. She was thorough, professional, and yet always amicable. Lisa even joined us for Mirador's Christmas celebration at a local restaurant.

It is best to let Lisa tell this story in her own words, and included below is Lisa's summary of how she approaches carbon projects and her assessment of Mirador. Lisa mentioned that her first impression of me was that I spoke a lot! No doubt I did because I was so pleased to talk about Mirador with someone knowledgeable, experienced, and insightful. I also had a funding challenge in the middle of the carbon bear market.

From Lisa, a story of carbon done correctly from the corporate perspective:

> What is the role of corporations in protecting our planet for future generations? This question has paved the way for the wave of corporate social responsibility over the last 20 years. Manufacturing goods, creating services, providing entertainment, and meeting the demands of consumers have driven business growth, leading to greater demand for natural resources and energy consumption to create products. As businesses grow, the trajectory has been growth in greenhouse gas emissions. However, my company had set a target to reduce our greenhouse gas emissions in half while marching toward a period of growth.

> The approach was to use resources efficiently, push innovation, and invest in solutions mother earth has provided for greenhouse gas (GHG) mitigation. This is investing in carbon projects to avoid and remove greenhouse gas emissions. Easier said than done. Although there are protocols for project development, the most challenging part was finding suitable projects and partners. There wasn't a handbook on how to select a carbon project, how to predict if the project will be successful or not, whether it is "additional," and whether the project is impactful.

> I came across projects that met the protocols, had the

documentation in place, completed Verification, and had plenty of marketing material with gorgeous photos of people smiling and adorable animals. Still, after a few meetings, they just didn't seem credible. Credible, as in additional, as in making a difference in the environment and to people. As meetings went on, the additionality piece didn't seem very additional. These were well-intentioned projects, with nothing "bad" about them, but they could not adequately substantiate the claim that they offered additional greenhouse gas reductions. Such projects may be excellent for pure philanthropy with the goal of conservation or development. But they do not fit the bill for claims of additional GHG reductions. I viewed the protocols for additionality tests as a starting point and would continue a barrage of questions to assess additionality. The issue with additionality—trying to determine intent.

My goal was to find projects that were not only additional but sustainable. Removal projects such as planting trees are the gold star, and we had those in our portfolio, but it takes 20–30 years for the trees to sequester a viable amount of carbon. We need to prevent more emissions from getting into the atmosphere now.

Back to finding projects, if the additional piece was there, then there was the program management side. Are these projects going to make it after year one? Do they have boots on the ground? Are they working with the community, and do the community members even want them there? I ask a lot of questions. How is the project communicated? How are benefits shared? Where are the offices, who manages them, what is their experience? Is the local government involved?

Again, nature-based projects, and projects working with communities, require more management than simply putting a methane gas capture over a landfill. However, getting a nature-based or community project launched has socioeconomic benefits and conservation value while also reducing GHGs.

The number of reputable project developers with experience in nature-based projects was minimal, and I needed to find more projects I could rely on. I started to expand my search to cookstoves projects. I wanted to invest in a project helping families utilize renewable fuels based on a scalable model. I was finally connected to Proyecto Mirador by an international NGO that Mirador was working with.

First impressions: Wow, this guy talks a lot, has a lot of passion and enthusiasm for the project, and has done quite a bit of research to develop a program, promising that there were a few stoves piloted.

After getting to know more about the project, I was impressed with the following:

- Operations on the ground in Honduras.

- Model of providing jobs, training, and sourcing locally for materials.

- Measurement, Reporting, and Verification.

- Attention to details.

- Constant desire to seek out efficiencies.

- Health benefits.

- Economic benefits.

- The passion of the Mirador team.

Honduras is not a country where our company has an operational presence or a high concentration of consumers of our product. The project was compelling enough in additionality, co-benefits, and management for us to make the initial investment. After the proven success of the initial investment, we returned to Mirador for successive investments and helped to scale the project beyond Honduras.

It is one of the projects I'm most proud of.

———————

Lisa's commitment to purchase Mirador carbon credits was a gratifying moment. But it wasn't just the sale of carbon credits that made this moment so significant. The value of carbon credits goes way beyond CO_2 tonnage and price. They are only the tip of the iceberg.

Notice the characteristics Lisa mentions in her assessment of Mirador: operations on the ground; providing jobs and training, and sourcing materials locally; quality of measurement, reporting, and verification; attention to detail; constant desire to innovate; health and economic benefits; passion. These are the steps a carbon project must climb to reach the Top of the Pyramid.

So no, it wasn't just the sale of carbon credits that made this moment so significant. Much more meaningful was that Lisa Shibata, one of the very best sustainability executives in the business, recognized, for the first time, the true value of the Mirador Model.

The Mirador Model: Aspire to Reach the Top of the Pyramid

"To be a model for how to do carbon projects, it takes tenacity, creativity, grit, patient investment and a steadfast vision."

—Stevan P. Simich, Founder and CEO, Mogli Technologies

Survive, learn, thrive

HARD WORK ALONE is not enough. Hard work must be guided by an overarching model.

We started building stoves in 2004 simply because we wanted to get smoke out of rural homes in a mountain valley in rural Central America. We built 29 stoves that year. More people came to us. So we built 2,000 stoves, then 5,000, then 10,000.

We had to create an organization capable of managing the growth. We struggled. We learned. We adapted. We survived. And ultimately, we thrived. With every success along the way, small or large, we were building a business prototype for Mirador and, unknowingly, for other carbon projects.

In 2013, Lisa Shibata was the first to recognize the value of the Mirador Model. Her support gave us confidence that we were on the right path. Confidence is empowering. The Mirador Model sustains us to this day as we pass 330,000 stoves in Central America.

The Mirador Model

I. Top of the Pyramid Project

- Create a quality product with high local demand.

- Embrace the best, most respected, most demanding certification of the project.

- Commit to transparency.

- Co-invest with stove owners.

- Self-finance growth to achieve independence.

II. Leadership Values

- Persistence

- Integrity

- Passion

- Aspirations

III. Global Best Practices

- Climate and Environmental: verified carbon reductions and reduced deforestation.

- Social benefits: health and economic benefits to homeowners, community job creation, training of employees, source materials locally, support small business formations.

- Practice innovation, investment, and improvement.

- Embrace a culture of diversity and inclusion.

IV. Long-Term Commitment

- 100% reinvestment of all carbon credit proceeds.

- Commitment to multi-generational leadership.

- A mission-based organization with long-term goals.

Is a model necessary for carbon projects?

There is sometimes a misconception that it is acceptable for philanthropic environmental projects, including carbon projects like Mirador, to be managed with a lower standard of rigor and discipline than commercial businesses. Having traveled with us in these chapters through Mirador's journey, you realize that is simply not true. Like any other business, carbon projects must be managed. And to do that, you need a business model.

Can a carbon project succeed without a business model? The story of Juan Orlando Hernandez, who became President of Honduras in 2013, will answer that question in the next chapter.

Even the President of Honduras Needs the Mirador Model

"No soy culpable." **"I am not guilty."**

—Former Honduran President Juan Orlando Hernandez, with chains around his ankles, pleading "not guilty" to U.S. drug and weapons charges in Manhattan federal court on May 10, 2022.

E NTERING 2013, WE felt confident. We were eager to continue growing and installing more great stoves in rural homes. We had proven the value of the Mirador Model.

Vida Mejor?

Then something happened that we could never have imagined. Juan Orlando Hernandez, leader of the Honduras National Congress, started a stove program of his own, funded by the government through a non-profit headed by his wife. Our initial reaction was to welcome another stove project. There would be even more stoves for Hondurans who needed them, less deforestation, and less CO_2 emitted into the atmosphere. All good.

However, shortly after announcing his stove project, Juan Orlando declared his candidacy for President of Honduras. This was the red flag that exposed his true motivation: to use the stove program as a political tool to secure votes from the rural poor. Despite the name of his stove initiative, Vida Mejor ("Better Life"), health and environmental benefits were not part of his agenda. He distributed a handful of his stoves in select rural villages so that he could extol his generosity and build popularity. His aspirations were purely political. The ploy worked: Juan Orlando won the presidency, in large part due to the rural vote.

Mirador is not political, so Juan Orlando never once spoke with us, never consulted us, never asked about our IT system or maps, and never even mentioned Mirador publicly. We could have helped, we were by far the biggest stove project in Honduras at the time, but he chose instead to ignore us. The whole experience of competing with a president of a country was surreal.

Juan Orlando had no business model to guide his stove program; he had an election to win.

You get what you vote for

Recall in the last chapter on the Mirador Model that having a quality product was at the top of the list. We learned from years of experience that if the stove doesn't work well, people won't use it. Juan Orlando chose a stove for his project that had never been used in Honduras: Envirofit. Nice name.

In contrast to Mirador's Dos por Tres, which is made of locally sourced materials, the components of Juan Orlando's stove were imported from China, consuming scarce foreign exchange reserves, and assembled in Honduras.

We encountered the first Juan Orlando stove in 2013 in a home near our headquarters in Santa Bárbara. We examined it and tested it. There were a few things about his stove that immediately concerned us. We could tell from the raw materials that it was expensive to manufacture and build, and would be expensive to maintain. It was a good-looking stove, but pretty doesn't count when stoves are used for seven hours a day, 365 days a year. The stoves were easily damaged, with many delicate parts that could not withstand the rigors of Honduran cooking. If there was one lesson we had learned over the years, it was that the stove's durability was absolutely essential.

Political rallies were held to celebrate the arrival of the stoves. Community politicians who were members of Juan Orlando's ruling National Party then decided who would receive the stoves and who wouldn't, always favoring their own constituents. Juan Orlando's program hired politically friendly personnel with no technical experience to deliver the stoves in boxes without any instructions for assembly, use, or maintenance.

The reception of Juan Orlando's stove by homeowners was predictable. Many families did not use them because the shape of the stove didn't fit their needs. Some complained about the stove's materials; for example, there were accidents involving burned children as the outside of the metal stove heated up to dangerous temperatures. Whether due to breakage or inconvenience, the stoves were soon relegated to serve as a table or desk while the old traditional stove continued to burn and fill houses with toxic smoke.

We even found Juan Orlando's stove in homes where we had already built a Dos por Tres. Some families took them because they were free and, being portable, they could be sold or given away. This made proper monitoring and maintenance of the stove nearly impossible since Juan Orlando's team had no idea where the stoves ended up. We shook our heads at this: monitoring and supervision were critical to ensuring the lasting success of the Dos por Tres.

As Mirador's technicians and supervisors ran into more and more of Juan Orlando's stoves in the field, they confirmed its failings and sent reports and photos back to our team in the office.

Juan Orlando's Report Card

Let's quickly grade Juan Orlando's stove project against the Mirador Model.

Create a Top of the Pyramid Project

- Juan Orlando's stove was unsuitable for use in rural Honduras. People didn't use it. Game over.
- Grade: **Fail**.

Global Best Practices

- Environmental and community benefits were never part of Juan Orlando's agenda.
- Grade: **Fail**.

Leadership Values

- Leadership values include persistence, integrity, passion, and aspirations. Juan Orlando? Integrity, no. For the other three, yes, but for all the wrong reasons.
- Grade: **Fail minus**.

Long-Term Commitment

- You have probably already guessed the answer, but we will get to that in a moment.

Climbing to the Top of the Pyramid is tough for any carbon project. Without a model to guide the project, it is impossible. Even with government money and the power of the presidential pulpit, Juan Orlando's project was doomed from the start.

Juan Orlando gives all
stoves a bad name

Juan Orlando's impact on Mirador and the Dos por Tres was disruptive in two ways.

First, Juan Orlando's stove program was promoted for all it was politically worth, backed by government money and his network of political cronies. Solicitations for the Dos por Tres dropped accordingly. Then, later, as the reputation of the government stove plummeted, there was the problem of association. Juan Orlando was giving all stoves a lousy name. Many rural homeowners began to erroneously equate Mirador with Juan Orlando's project and his failed stove, unfairly eroding Mirador's reputation. Explaining this, and rebuilding trust in the Dos por Tres, had to be done house by house, community by community.

The great shame of Juan Orlando's stove program was that, before it began, Honduras already had in place one of the most successful stove projects in the Global South. Mirador was cash flow positive; we were managed by Hondurans; we required no assistance from the government; and we built durable stoves from locally sourced materials that were appropriate for local cooking conditions and practices.

It was a frustrating time at Mirador. Our program was working well, but we spent an inordinate amount of time circumventing the confusion Juan Orlando had created.

But things would turn our way. In 2017, Honduras had another presidential election which had an unexpected impact on Mirador.

Caught stealing second

While Juan Orlando's political cronies were promoting their stove program in the countryside, Juan Orlando himself was busy in the capital engineering his presidential future. He seemed to have everything in place to win re-election in 2017.

Alas, on election night, the voting didn't go his way. With 57% of the votes, Juan Orlando trailed by five percentage points. Desperate, he ordered that vote counting be suspended. When the counting proceeded 36 hours later, Juan Orlando—surprise, surprise—was pronounced the winner. But you cannot fool Hondurans. Widespread rioting broke out. Roads were blocked, and businesses closed. And even when the rioting was eventually quelled, widespread anger lingered. Juan Orlando's presidency never regained legitimacy.

The good news is that, amidst his mounting troubles, Juan Orlando exited the presidency and the stove business. So much for Vida Mejor's long-term commitment.

With Juan Orlando's departure in January 2022, demand for Mirador's stoves once again took off, and Juan Orlando took off in a U.S. State Department jet bound for jail in Rikers Island, extradited on drug-trafficking and weapons charges. In 2022 alone Mirador built 55,000 stoves, more than double our previous annual record.

A cookstove provided by Vida Mejor and cast aside by its recipient.

Mirador Establishes Leadership

"It is amazing what you can accomplish if you do not care who gets the credit."

—Harry S. Truman

WE HAVE BEEN working on stoves for 19 years. We have come a long way from our humble beginnings in Atima. We have described in these chapters many of our efforts to transform Mirador from an informal effort to install stoves into a great carbon project.

Has the Mirador Model succeeded? Is Mirador a Top of the Pyramid project? You decide. Here are the facts:

Scale

Mirador has built over 330,000 stoves as of 2023. It took us 11 years to build the first 100,000 stoves. It took us five years to build the second 100,000 stoves. It took us only two years to build the most recent 100,000 stoves.

We have provided over 500 million clean cooking days to 1.6 million people in Central America.

We have extended our work across Honduras and now into Guatemala. We are the leading project of its kind in Central America.

Adaptation

Chepe and Santos, our first stove builders in 2004, struggled to read or write. Fast forward four years, in 2008 we showed up with iPhones and Notebooks and found that many of our employees had never held one, let alone used one. Today, we operate with a comprehensive, integrated electronic system in which all 250 employees are fully and proudly online.

We have collected 600,000 surveys, recorded at least as many GPS marks to confirm our stove locations, and carried out over 1,450 Kitchen Performance Tests. Our supervisors have made 1.3 million follow-up visits to the homes of our clients.

We don't adopt technology for its own sake or the sake of mere modernism. We invest in technology because it makes us better at what we do, improves the quality of our work, and allows us to reach more people than would otherwise be possible.

Carbon reductions

Every stove we build reduces carbon emissions by 15 tonnes over five years. In our 19 years of operation, our stoves have reduced carbon emissions by over three million tonnes.

Mirador was the fourth cookstove project in the world to attain Gold Standard Certification. Our carbon reductions are verified, measured, and trusted.

We have a list of respected buyers for our carbon credits, which resonate worldwide by providing corporations with a way to offset their emissions.

We have sold over $25 million of carbon credits and invested 100% of the proceeds into the project.

Social benefits

Care for the rural poor is at the core of our vision. The social benefits of our stove are paramount, not just carbon credits.

By constantly investing and reinvesting, we direct capital to help the people who need it most in communities where help would not otherwise reach.

When two hurricanes struck Honduras in November 2020, Mirador temporarily stopped building stoves so that we could deliver humanitarian aid to communities badly impacted by the storms. This is who we are.

Employment

We provide jobs to over 250 people and our work sustains 39 small businesses in the communities where we work.

We have expanded our office staff. We invest in training and education. University graduates continue to join us, which we take as a sign of the success of Mirador and our culture.

We give opportunities to young people and guide them in their growth. Our staff includes people of all educational levels.

We have groomed the second generation of leadership under Engineer Rafael Mendoza, Doña Emilia's son. When Rafael joined us in early 2019, he put our growth into overdrive.

If only the government of Honduras could have humble and effective leadership like Doña Emilia, Professor Elder, and Engineer Rafael.

Our culture

We have created a strong Mirador Culture.

We believe success is built upon dedication to quality and excellence, and total commitment to our clients, staff, and suppliers.

We value all of our collaborators, and we treat them with the same respect as our employees.

We consciously avoid discrimination based on ethnicity, politics, religion, or sexual preference. We always aim to be inclusive and open our doors to anyone who identifies with our ideals.

Quicken the journey

We do not state these facts about Mirador to congratulate ourselves, but rather to share what we have learned with others. We encourage others to join our movement to help people cook with clean stoves and save our climate. We hope this book will quicken their journey to the Top of the Pyramid.

The journey to the Top of the Pyramid is constantly evolving. And as more and more projects aspire to generate high-integrity carbon credits, our collective standards and achievements will rise. That is a good thing because, as we describe in Part Three of this book, we all need to be at the Top of the Pyramid to accomplish what must be done for each other and our climate.

Improvements to the Dos por Tres

Here are a few of the physical improvements we made to the Dos por Tres over the years:

- Optimized dimensions of the *plancha* (cooktop) to maximize thermal efficiency.

- Strengthened the *plancha* with *parches* (patches) at either end to extend serviceable life.

- Dee's Corner: Redesigned the brick assembly to avoid cracking in the corners of the stove.

- Added a *parrilla* (grate) to raise firewood off the stove base and increase air flow.

- Invented El Cinco to perform the five steps necessary for stove maintenance.

- Created a Use and Maintenance Brochure with pictorial instructions for the five maintenance steps.

- Added a plaque with a hook to hang El Cinco and brochure right by the stove.

- Increased the thickness of the chimney.

Honduran woman and her Dos por Tres with all the upgrades, plaque with El Cinco, and Use and Maintenance Brochure hanging on the wall.

Mirador senior management in 2023 (L–R): Professor Elder Mendoza Mejia, Director of Operations; Doña Emilia Giron de Mendoza, Executive Director; and Rafael Mendoza, Director of International Operations.

Mirador
Photo Well

Hondurans wait patiently outside the clinic in Atima.

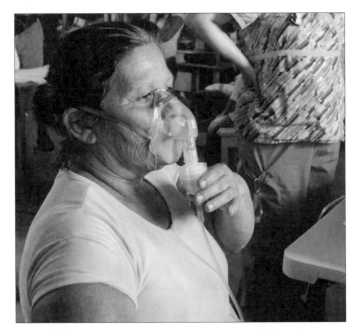

A woman breathes through a nebulizer at the clinic in Atima.

Traditional stove belches smoke into the kitchen.

Smoke envelops the pot as it struggles to simmer on this inefficient stove.

A traditional stove with corner walls blackened by its smoke.

Flames pouring out of this traditional stove underline its inefficiency.

Mirador finds a solution: Don Santos, Mirador's first employee,
stands by a stove under construction.

Mirador *Ejecutor* Omar Mejia educates community members on the stove.

"The stove is very good, it heats up faster, I cook the tortillas quickly."
—Anmy Yoselin Ramos, family of three, Copan, Honduras.

The Dos por Tres stove provides variable heat to cook tortillas
while multiple pots simmer.

"The thing I like most about this stove is that we don't inhale smoke;
it would be good if every person were able to have this stove."
—Maria Margarita Hernandez, family of five, Intibuca, Honduras.

A woman shows pride of ownership in her improved cookstove.
No Cuesta, No Cuida.

An elderly woman and her granddaughter are tasked
with collecting wood.

A Honduran man cuts fuel wood for cooking.

A boy peeks in to see his next meal simmering.

A Honduran woman carries her new *plancha* home.

PART THREE

Great Carbon Projects Require Cool Effect

The Problem of Climate Change for the World

November 6, 2012: "The concept of global warming was created by and for the Chinese in order to make U.S. manufacturing non-competitive."

September 26, 2016: "I did not—I did not—I do not say that. I do not say that 'climate change is a hoax perpetrated by the Chinese.'"

—Donald J. Trump

C LIMATE CHANGE IS happening. The science is clear. Today's urgent debate is not about the science of climate change but about what we can do to reduce our carbon emissions.

Doing so, however, is the hard part. Everywhere we look, in everything we research, we learn how challenging it is for individuals and corporations to shrink their carbon footprint.

Individuals

What can we change in our daily lives to reduce our carbon footprint?

The first steps are easy. Buy renewable energy from your local utility company. Replace all the lighting in your house with LED bulbs, of course. Recycle, absolutely. Turn your heat down a few degrees, sure. Stop eating meat, cut out dairy? Reduce them, at least. You start with these steps, but they are small steps that only nip at the margin.

What else can we do?

Drive less? OK, but how do we get around to all the places we must go daily? Walk or ride your bike, if possible, but most modern cities were built for automobiles. If you live in Atlanta or Houston or Los Angeles—or, for that matter, in almost any major city worldwide—your commute is probably far too long for cycling or walking to be practical. And public mass transit in most cities is woefully inadequate.

How about flying? Video calls are great, but there are occasions when travel is unavoidable and necessary. You cannot walk or ride your bike from San Francisco to Hong Kong. You might fly less often, but there will be times when you still need to fly. For transportation, those are the options. That's it.

In your home, you can rip out your walls and install insulation. Or you can install solar panels on your roof. But wait, this is getting expensive. I'll plan on it, but maybe next year or after the kids leave college…

Let's take this to the extreme to see how far we can go. Sell your house and car, and live homeless on the streets: *your carbon footprint is still eight tonnes.*

So, even then, we still haven't solved climate change. And, back in the real world, the fact is that the average American has a 16-tonne carbon footprint.

Ten years ago, I asked my colleagues in Hong Kong to buy carbon credits to offset their personal emissions. One bright analyst told me he would buy a few houseplants for his porch instead. When I asked him for the accounting, his research showed there was no balcony in Hong Kong big enough to offset his emissions with houseplants. He was well paid, but not *that* well paid.

At the end of the day, it is not realistic to expect that people will stop flying, driving, eating meat, or heating their homes. The fact is that reducing emissions is difficult and expensive.

Corporate emissions

For corporations, identifying and measuring the scope of their emissions can be mind-bending.

Corporate emissions are woven into our globalized world in a huge tapestry of interconnected global activities. There are Scope 1 emissions from direct operations. There are Scope 2 emissions from the electricity needed for lights, servers, and computers. And there are Scope 3 emissions from a company's upstream supply chain and the downstream use of its products. If it is challenging for companies to calculate whose Scope 3 emissions are whose, then it is nearly impossible to accurately measure a company's overall emissions.

Corporations were never set up to minimize CO_2 emissions. They were the beneficiaries of the inexpensive energy of the past 140 years. They never had to pay for the consequences of their emissions, nor for the cost of mitigating the climate change they caused.

As the need to address climate change has risen in the public mind, corporations have started to take note. Some companies took the easy route by making empty statements about "responsibility" and spent more on public relations than on actually cutting emissions. Greenwashing was easy in a world where the fossil fuel industry and climate deniers politicized climate change. And companies made false statements, overstating their emission reductions by exaggerating their baseline emissions. Seeing this was not a surprise, but it has made the problem tougher to resolve.

Then there are the many companies that promise to be "Net Zero by 2050." For too many CEOs, "Net Zero by 2050" is just a way of kicking the can down the road, leaving the problem for the next CEO, or hoping that some future technology might soon be discovered to make the problem go away. "Net Zero by 2050" sounds great, but the question is: How are you going to do that? What are you doing today to reach that goal?

Thankfully, other companies took climate change very seriously and tried to decarbonize, but discovered that with technologies available today, they were able to achieve the reduction of just a modest percentage of their overall emissions. The number of fully engaged corporations is growing, but we need more corporates to engage in this fight.

A good question

We know how hard it is for individuals and corporations to reduce their emissions. Should we do nothing and wait for a future solution to bail us out?

No.

The world needs everyone working on every possible solution and every technology, but even with urgency, the shift will take time. What can we do *now* to accelerate things? What can we do *today* to make a difference?

Well, for a start, in addition to reducing operational emissions wherever possible, we can buy high-integrity carbon credits to offset our emissions.

For example, every Dos por Tres stove in Central America reduces carbon emissions by three tonnes yearly, and we have built over 330,000 stoves. That is a lot of carbon. And carbon credits make that happen. Mirador today is only financially possible because like-minded individuals and companies buy Mirador's carbon credits.

However, Mirador is small in the greater scheme of climate change. We cannot possibly scale to anything close to what the world requires. Sometimes at Mirador, we laugh and ask: How many Miradors would it take to make a significant difference in climate change? That is a scary question.

But maybe it is a good question. Are there more Miradors out there? Are there other great carbon-reducing projects? Where? How many? Are there enough to make a difference? Will there be more?

My wife Dee and I had this very conversation one memorable evening. We need a new chapter to tell this story.

Welcome to Cool Effect

"Earth, we're here. Join us."

—Cool Effect

One memorable evening

ONE EVENING AT home, over a glass of wine, my wife Dee and I reflected on our experiences at Proyecto Mirador. We remarked on how much the world had changed and how our Mirador mission had grown.

We had begun building stoves in Honduras to help people remove toxic smoke from their homes. As awareness of climate change had arisen from obscurity to centrality, our mission had grown from a local community project to carbon reductions that could help the planet. We had successfully created a carbon emission reduction project that helped us go from building 1,500 stoves a year to 5,000 stoves, then to 18,000 stoves, and eventually to 55,000 stoves in 2022. And the world needed many more growing carbon-reduction projects.

At Mirador, we had been fortunate over the years that exceptional people like Doña Emilia, Professor Elder, Engineer Rafael, and *Ejecutor* Fredy had helped Mirador survive and thrive. We had been lucky that Jeremy

Grantham had supported us financially when we needed it most, and had opened our eyes to the challenges and responsibilities of climate change, and the opportunity for carbon credits. And just as we had been helped by so many, maybe we could help others, too.

Over the years, we had personally come to know other dedicated entrepreneurs running carbon reduction projects around the world. We knew that carbon finance was transformative to these projects, delivering tangible benefits to disadvantaged communities, and that they were struggling, as Mirador once had, just to survive.

The threat of climate change was becoming more real with every passing day, and we knew that having a market for carbon credits had to take on greater importance in the coming years if humanity was to slow global warming. The problem was that the multi-year bear market in carbon had made it even more difficult for carbon projects, just at a time when they were needed most. It was frustrating.

What help could we offer? We knew what it took to create a good carbon project. We had experience in carbon credits and with carbon buyers. "And we know that people are looking for a way to do something about climate change," Dee said. The idea was forming.

And so it was that, over a second glass of wine, our conversation became more animated and we decided to set up a non-profit entity to help heighten awareness and mobilize capital for the entrepreneurial developers who were reducing CO_2 emissions on the back of carbon finance.

Thus was the founding of Cool Effect.

What's in a name?

Why the name "Cool Effect"? Think of the Butterfly Effect, the Snowball Effect, or the Domino Effect. In a similar way, the Cool Effect is one small action to stop global warming, amplified by many people, accumulating to create a movement for positive change. That is the Cool Effect. For us, it was the perfect name. And the logo was equally great.

The Cool Effect Logo says it well.

Know your mission

We didn't yet have a business model for Cool Effect. That would come with time. But for now, we needed a clear mission statement:

> The goal of Cool Effect is to deliver high-quality credits to support great carbon emission reduction projects and to help educate the world on how to distinguish between actual emission savings and greenwashing.

An honored colleague

We also needed good people to help us fulfill the Cool Effect mission. The first person we called was Siddharth "Sid" Yadav, Global Technical Manager for SGS, where he was the technical lead for SGS's country offices regarding climate change mitigation project assessments. SGS is one of the world's leading testing, inspection, and certification companies.

We met Sid when he worked at SGS and performed Mirador's first Gold Standard site visit for Verification. We knew that he had traveled the world auditing the good, the bad, and the ugly of carbon projects. He was an encyclopedia of knowledge about the minutia of carbon accounting and the whole range of existing carbon reduction methodologies.

But what really attracted us to Sid was that he genuinely cared. Certainly, he was tough on assessing additionality, leakage, permanence, and the accuracy of emission claims. But Sid also cared about the quality of management, the durability of the project, and especially the community benefits. He shared our passion for supporting great projects. When we described to him our idea for Cool Effect, he embraced the mission immediately.

Shortly after that, Sid joined Cool Effect, and we set him loose in search of more great projects. As expected, he delivered. Sid understood the Mirador Model and had a keen eye for identifying Top of the Pyramid projects. And while he traveled all across the Global South, the rest of us at Cool Effect were working to mobilize a movement. So many people, we believed, were looking for a way to help fight climate change. So many carbon projects needed financial support. Carbon projects plus individuals, by joining together, could help the planet. That story begins in the next chapter.

A Strategy to
Help Projects

"Success is not final. Failure is not fatal. It is the courage to continue that counts."

Six Americas

DURING OUR EFFORTS in 2014 to mobilize resources for great carbon projects, we became intrigued by the research of Professor Anthony Leiserowitz at the Yale School of Climate Change Communications.

In surveys of a nationally representative sample of American adults, Professor Leiserowitz studied American attitudes toward climate change, including their beliefs, policy preferences, and climate-relevant behaviors. The data is categorized into a progressive range of opinions called "The Six Americas: Alarmed, Concerned, Cautious, Disengaged, Doubtful, and Dismissive."

At one end of the spectrum are the Alarmed, who are convinced that global warming is happening, human-caused, an urgent threat, and who strongly support climate policies. At the other end of the spectrum are the Dismissive who believe global warming is not happening, human-caused, or a threat, most of whom endorse conspiracy theories such as: "global warming is a hoax invented by the Chinese." The survey is repeated annually to track the shifting proportions amongst the six groups.

The following diagram illustrates the proportion of the survey respondents in each of these six groups in October 2014.

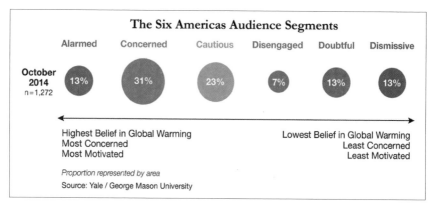

American attitudes toward global warming in 2014, the basis for Cool Effect's outreach to individuals as buyers of carbon credits.

Two Americas

The Alarmed and Concerned groups caught our attention. These individuals are most engaged with the issue and most supportive of climate solutions.

Professor Leiserowitz's research suggested that at that time, in 2014, 44% of Americans identified as Alarmed or Concerned. That's nearly 140 million people; the group's sheer size was compelling. The research further confirmed that these groups were highly active on Facebook and other social media platforms.

In March 2015, we hired Ogilvy, a global advertising firm, to help us mobilize the Alarmed and Concerned to buy carbon credits to offset their carbon footprint. Ogilvy surveyed 450 respondents and reported the following:

- 74% of the Alarmed and 51% of the Concerned reported having a high interest in natural resource preservation.

- 62% of the Alarmed and 43% of the Concerned said they would be interested in buying an offset.

- Among those surveyed, 66% would consider offsets as a gift.

- 95% of Alarmed and 90% of Concerned would tell their friends about their own offsetting.

- Both groups were surprised that it would only cost $150 to offset their carbon footprint for a year.

One strategy

Ogilvy advised Cool Effect to connect directly with the 140 million Alarmed and Concerned individuals keen to do more on climate change. Their research gave us confidence that we could create a movement among these people to take action to neutralize their carbon footprint by purchasing carbon credits. How large might the movement grow? How many projects could be helped? If we could convince 100 people to buy credits, why not 1,000? And if 1,000, why not 10,000?

Cielo, the young woman who identified the need for clean cookstoves in Honduras a decade earlier, officially launched our campaign at COP21 in Paris in 2015, a massive global conference held each year when the world's attention turns to climate change. We sold 142 credits at the Paris launch. Three months later, we sold our 143rd credit. The lack of transactions was a warning sign, but in our enthusiasm, we ignored the storm clouds far away on the horizon.

2016 was the year of testing and learning what messages would engage individuals and get them involved in climate change. We turned to social media and its hundreds of millions of users. Research promoted the effectiveness of social media. If we could create a movement on social media, sales of carbon credits would surely follow. It seemed so simple:

individuals could click the link to Cool Effect's website, select a project, and offset their emissions.

We started broadly by looking at basic phrases. Would "global warming" or "climate change" get more attention? Neither was the answer. Americans responded to simplicity and ease. Cool Effect began to talk about climate as a movement. "Earth, we're here. Join us." was the language that drove people to click consistently for years. They also responded to weather. When we combined posts with current weather conditions, we would see a spike in responses. This could relate to heat, drought, and rising sea levels in the context of climate.

But none of the ads performed as well as those that were irreverent. "Make Doo Doo Do More," for instance, Cool Effect's title for a biogas methane capture project, was a huge favorite. Americans finally felt that they had a brand that made climate accessible and understandable.

As the months and quarters passed, however, it became evident that our strategy to create a movement of individuals was at once a smashing success—and a dismal failure. We attracted a fantastic 500,000 people to sign on to the Cool Effect movement. But only a handful of carbon credits were purchased. We got the clicks but not the sales.

Though morally motivated, the Alarmed and Concerned individuals clearly didn't want to buy credits. They seemed to say, "Climate change is something for the government or corporations to handle," or "I already recycle and have changed my lightbulbs." Facebook and Google, owners of the dominant social media platforms at that time, loved Cool Effect's persistence and were happy to take our money.

How small is .003%?

Nowhere was our failure more evident than in a video we created entitled *Save Our Snowmen*, an engaging mockumentary highlighting the impact of climate change on our beloved snowmen.

The video launched on Giving Tuesday, November 30, 2016, and garnered even more attention than we could have imagined. On Facebook, the campaign achieved a very high click-through rate of 4.11% (average = 1.84%). Across all platforms, the average click-through rate was an excellent 3.92%. YouTube alone drew over 7,000,000 views. The video also received creativity awards from Graphis and Communication Arts and a feature story in *Adweek*. By the time the campaign ended in April 2017, it had generated a remarkable 13,431,428 views.

Our problem was that all of those views generated a meager 421 transactions.

That's correct: 13.4 million views and 421 transactions, a minuscule success rate of .003%. Sales revenues of $31,559 were less than the cost of the campaign.

We had learned a harsh lesson about individuals' indifference to taking action to offset their carbon emissions, and our goal to help the project developers had hit a wall. We had to face the hard fact that creating a social media movement to generate sales was a broken proposition. With these painful numbers, we were staring at yet another Valley of Death in our effort to slow climate change.

Below are some screen shots from the mockumentary. Perhaps you will visit YouTube (search: "Save Our Snowmen") and join the 13.4 million others who enjoyed the video. Or—better yet—join the relatively infinitesimal number of individuals who offset their carbon on the Cool Effect website.

When asked how lunch was, migrating snowmen replied,
"We'd give it two thumbs up if we had thumbs."

Gus Evans, owner of "Beverages and More," tries to support the snow people
who stop in his store, but lately some of them are wearing out their welcome.

An appeal for help from Lula Larsson of Holiday Hills who is looking for her lost snowman, Mr. Flakes. If you find him, she is requesting that you keep him cold.

Local farmers report that migrating snowmen are picking up their pace in an effort to avoid losing more mass.

Back to the drawing board

Cool Effect's business model was successful among the project developers who were generating high-quality carbon credits. Our experience at Mirador and the creation of the Mirador Model informed our ability to select great projects. But we hadn't yet identified buyers. Our well-researched but failed social media campaigns were our first attempt to create a business model for the buyer's side of the carbon market. Our aspirations were correct, but our strategy was flawed.

We needed to go back to the drawing board. We had to figure this out. Climate change was still threatening.

The Cool
Effect Pivot

"I believe the role carbon credits should play in any corporate climate strategy is 'last but not later,' meaning that, first, we want to reduce our emissions in every way possible, then think about compensating for any emissions that cannot be avoided or reduced."

—Patrick Flynn, Global Head of Sustainability, Salesforce

THE IDEA OF creating a carbon credit movement among individuals had seemed promising. Its failure was a brutal reckoning for us. Maybe we just needed to change our approach. There must be some way to communicate with 140 million people, all claiming to want to act on climate change. There must be a way to make this work.

It was difficult to relinquish the idea, but we had to face the fact that creating a social media movement to generate sales was a broken proposition.

Jodi gets us back on track

Jodi Manning, Director of Marketing at Cool Effect, helped to get us back on track. She suggested we consider the corporate market. Cool

Effect's strength was our ability to identify and analyze great carbon projects. But would corporations need us? "I know some of the people on the sustainability team at Salesforce," Jodi said. We were familiar with Salesforce. Proyecto Mirador used their database software in our operations in Honduras. We were their first non-profit Salesforce customer in Central America. "And I know they utilize carbon credits to offset their emissions," she said.

Shortly afterward, we met with Patrick Flynn, who was then the Global Head of Sustainability at Salesforce, along with Max Scher, then the company's Sustainability Manager. The meeting went well. Patrick expressed interest in visiting the Mirador project. Nothing sells the value of carbon credits like personally visiting homes in the rural communities of Honduras backed up by the Salesforce database of surveys, maps, and evidence of stove use.

Soon afterward, Max visited Honduras and Salesforce became the first major corporate client of Cool Effect. They came along at the right time, giving us confidence in our mission. They recognized the value of the Cool Effect Model even before we did.

Just as important, however, was that Patrick helped us to understand his mission as a sustainability officer. His sophisticated approach gave us insight into the willingness of a growing number of corporations to take responsible action on climate change and the expertise and intelligence that some companies dedicated to the mission. In the following section Patrick Flynn describes the role of carbon credits in the Salesforce climate strategy.

"Because it is the right thing to do."

Salesforce has been on its climate action journey for over a decade, and it is not done. Our leadership team acknowledged the climate emergency, and we have chosen to move quickly. We ask, "How fast can we accelerate our emission reductions, 100% renewable, and net emissions commitments without sacrificing quality?"

Acceleration

Achieving renewable energy goals is not going to happen overnight. It takes time, and we will only move as fast as quality will allow. But, since the planet cannot wait, we will continue to prioritize emissions reductions first and will compensate fully for all emissions that we cannot avoid or reduce with carbon credits. For example, we began accelerating our renewable energy goals as fast as we could in 2015, and we hit our target in 2020. Contrast that to our use of high-integrity carbon credits, which allowed us to act immediately to meet our net emissions goals without sacrificing quality.

That's where Cool Effect comes into the picture. We saw in Proyecto Mirador a few things that we liked. One was the emphasis on transparent quality measurement. Also very special was the focus on co-benefits for the local communities. Going down to Honduras and seeing the respiratory problems caused by traditional stoves prompted us to look more deeply at social co-benefits. Carbon offset projects bring capital to areas of the world most impacted by the climate crisis, and high-quality, well-designed projects provide significant positive co-benefits to affected regional communities.

Last but not later

Emissions reduction is always the most important first step in any company's Net Zero journey. But carbon credits also play an important role in enabling the world to move closer to Net Zero.

Critics claim that carbon credits allow polluters to "buy their way" out of accountability, but in reality, they are a positive tool at a time when all essential tools need to be used with expert precision as fast as possible. The urgency of the environmental crisis demands an all-of-the-above mindset when it comes to taking action.

It is also true that not all carbon credits are equally beneficial. But more and more companies—including Salesforce—have rigorous standards for evaluating potential carbon credit purchases and seek out high-quality carbon credits to compensate for emissions they cannot yet reduce. It will continue to be critical for Salesforce, and any other company taking bold climate action, to be transparent about how carbon offset projects are evaluated and selected.

I believe the role carbon credits should play in any corporate climate strategy is "last but not later," meaning that, first, we want to reduce our emissions in every way possible, then think about compensating for any emissions that cannot be avoided or reduced. Any company with a Net Zero by 2050 goal (or 2040 or 2030) knows they will eventually have to pull on the carbon credit lever. There is no logic in waiting. We can utilize the highest quality carbon credits today to accelerate tomorrow's Net Zero commitments, transitioning to full carbon removal credits over time.

A Cool Effect Model?

Our experience with Salesforce showed us that Cool Effect had a positive role to play in the corporate world. Our ability to identify high-quality carbon projects matched corporate needs to purchase verifiably high-quality carbon credits. A Cool Effect business model was coming into focus.

But corporate activism on climate change was still in its early days; more the exception than the norm. The prolonged bear market in carbon would end only when enough buyers embraced the value of high-quality carbon credits. Patrick Flynn, and others like him, understood that carbon credits are an essential part of the climate change solution. When would the rest of the world wake up to this fact?

The Bear Market for Carbon Ends

"Sustainability doesn't mean sacrificing profits or putting success on the back burner. Instead, it has become a crucial element to any organization's successful strategy."

—Harvard Business School, Business Insights

I N 2021, THE carbon bear market mercifully came to an end.

There are many explanations for why bear markets end, but exhaustion is always high on the list. And the Cool Effect team was exhausted. We were able to hold on only because we believed in our mission; we had partnerships with an array of high-quality carbon developers who believed in Cool Effect and acknowledgment by at least some corporate buyers who valued our work.

However, with a few exceptions like Salesforce, the corporate world seemed indifferent to climate change. The indifference was confounding. The climate science was becoming harder to deny; the drumbeat of climate news was ever-present in our lives through fires, floods, hurricanes, and heatwaves. Yet people still seemed to think of climate change as someone else's problem, or something the government would take care of someday.

Wall Street weighs in

In the midst of all that indifference, though, something significant was happening on Wall Street: ESG investing (Environmental, Social & Governance). Climate risk was beginning to be recognized as investment risk, and corporate ESG policies became a focus of attention in the financial world. Nothing mobilizes corporate action like unified investor activism.

Wall Street, always eager to sell a story, jumped on the idea by creating ESG products for investors. Investment funds were established with share portfolios of corporations whose ESG policies were deemed socially and environmentally responsible. No one took advantage of the trend more than Larry Fink, CEO of Blackrock, though he is perhaps better known for his sharp eye for business opportunities than for his concern about the climate. When Larry expanded the Blackrock ESG funds, other investors worldwide jumped on the ESG bandwagon. Corporate executives, with their ESG policies now scrutinized, had to pay attention. And just like that, the carbon credit bear market was over.

The end of the bear market in carbon coincided with society's rising awareness of the urgency of climate change. Still, the newfound interest in ESG investing on Wall Street was a key climate accelerant for the corporate world. Larry Fink's salesmanship, although controversial, has ultimately had a positive impact on the environment by forcing public corporations to address climate change. And as corporations were forced to respond, so ended the bear market for carbon credits.

It was a game changer for the Cool Effect team, who could now offer solutions to a corporate market that was finally starting to listen.

The SBTi Trap

In a rush to respond to the new demands posed by ESG requirements, corporates searched for action that would show their pedigree. This is where the Science Based Targets initiative ("SBTi") came in. It was funded by the World Resources Institute (WRI), the Worldwide Fund for Nature (WWF), and CDP, the carbon accounting non-profit. SBTi executives came up with a great idea that corporations should declare they will have Net Zero emissions by 2050. Net Zero by 2050 was a perfect solution for many CEOs. They could pay lip service to their commitment to solving their emissions problem, but in some undetermined way, and in a timeframe that well surpassed the current CEO's responsibility.

CEOs, if they chose, could make future promises over emission reductions that required no real action today. The emission reductions would happen someday in the future, under someone else's watch, when they were in happy retirement.

What these complacent executives did not understand was that ESG investing and SBTi were about to change the playbook for corporations. In 2022, SBTi added a clever requirement to the Net Zero by 2050 commitment, that corporates must set and disclose their short- and intermediate-term targets for reducing emissions. Stakeholders demanded that corporations show their climate plans are tangible, credible, and transparent. Suddenly, that faraway 2050 horizon got much, much closer. This was the SBTi Trap—and by the end of 2022, more than 5,000 companies had fallen into it.

"Houston, we have a problem"

CEOs, taken aback by the sudden need for transparency and accountability, struggled to come to terms with the enormity of the task. The demands of shareholders, activists, and NGOs forced many corporations to confront the reality of decarbonizing their operations for the first time. Stakeholders set a high bar, with no room for greenwashing or false claims.

You could almost hear the raised voices in corporate executive suites responding to stakeholders:

"What do you mean, where is my 2025 Plan? Let me get back to you on that."

"Hold on. You are considering submitting a shareholder resolution to demand a 2025 Plan??!!"

"OK, I get it that we need to purchase renewable energy. We can do that. But now you say we must actually build renewable energy facilities and incur capital expenditures? Where will the capital come from?"

"Let me try to understand this. We need to reduce our emissions with technology that hasn't even been developed yet. How do we do that? And how much is this going to cost us?"

As corporations began to grapple with this harsh new reality, a new vocabulary entered the business world. Terms like Net Zero Commitments, Scope 3 Emissions, Carbon Adjusted EPS, Carbon Intensity of Businesses, Social Cost of Carbon, Non-Abatable Emissions, Additionality, Leakage, and Permanence became common jargon. New departments were established, such as Corporate Sustainability and Net Zero. Heavy emitting industries were identified and targeted for particular scrutiny, including Oil and Gas, Cement, Steel, Autos, Heavy Vehicles, Dairy, Agriculture, Landfills, and Waste.

Employees and customers also began to demand action as the new generation of workers and consumers became increasingly conscious of the need to protect the environment and reduce adaptation costs.

And meanwhile, Larry Fink's ESG assets under management continued to soar along with his share price as climate awareness and activism spread. More and more Americans, whether they realized it or not, were joining the long-awaited Cool Effect Movement.

The phones start ringing at Cool Effect

As Sustainability Officers calculated the size of the problem, it became clear that achieving emission reduction targets over the next three decades would be a daunting task, and one that would come at a significant cost.

Corporations also began to realize that achieving their emission reduction targets required a radical overhaul of procedures, systems, and technologies. This would take time. In the interim, carbon credits could be used to achieve the desired goals while their emissions were being reduced. The result was that demand for carbon credits began to rise.

Phones started ringing around the world as companies like Apple Computer and Unilever called their suppliers and demanded to see their 2025 plans. In contrast, fossil fuel companies and other heavy emitters began calling their public relations agencies to construct their next disinformation campaign.

For the first time, stakeholders could see how corporations were acting in response to climate change. Were they genuinely interested in reducing emissions, or were their claims false or misleading? Were they interested in greenwashing with cheap non-additional credits, or were they engaged in real operational change and high-quality carbon offsets?

Faced with such scrutiny, corporations began contacting Cool Effect, and we emerged as a trusted piece of the solution. Predictably, the companies most assertive in implementing their operational reductions understood the proper role of carbon credits in their strategy and were the most active buyers of carbon credit offsets. But high-quality carbon credits are complicated. Companies needed to know that what they were buying was reliable, making a meaningful impact, and verifiably reducing carbon.

Excellent points

Integrity, also, was beginning to come to the fore. The best companies sought transparency and trust, and they bought only the highest quality carbon credits with the most reliable methodologies. They demanded rigorous environmental and social benefits. Their requirements were right in our wheelhouse. We welcomed them and applauded them. The Cool Effect Model, in all its dimensions, was at last finding its place.

The Cool Effect Model: Carbon Done Correctly

"In order to do something, you must be something."

—Admiral James Stockdale, the longest-serving and
highest-ranking American POW during the Vietnam War

OVER THE YEARS, Cool Effect has executed great marketing campaigns to create a climate movement around individuals. But for the corporate world, we needed a professionalized analytical approach to guide clients to appropriate opportunities in the Voluntary Carbon Market. We drafted the first version of what has since become known as the Cool Effect Model.

Here is that Model:

I. Project Selection

Cool Effect performs rigorous due diligence as follows:

- Select projects with robust methodologies that confirm Additionality, Permanence, Leakage, and Baselines.

- Ensure transparent use of proceeds.

- Conduct site visits to understand the quantification of social benefits.

- Offer professionalism from 19 years of experience as developers, buyers, and climate philanthropists to create value for both projects and clients.

II. Management with Integrity

- Be a mission-based organization, not profit-driven.
- Align interests of Top of the Pyramid buyers with Top of the Pyramid developers.
- Explore the expansive universe of projects, but accept only a limited number of the very best.
- Limit the number of clients at Cool Effect to ensure quality and long-term partnerships.

III. Commit to Best Business Practices

- Legally provide transparency of pricing to both buyer and seller.
- Limit Cool Effect markup to 9.87% on every tonne.
- Outlaw greed in the business practices of all parties.

IV. Long-Term Vision

- Create genuine partnerships with clients who are committed to long-term decarbonization.
- Protect the reputation of our clients with quality projects.
- Execute the mission of educating all participants in the Voluntary Carbon Market.

As more corporations followed Salesforce to Cool Effect, we realized that the components of the Cool Effect Model were the reason. The Cool Effect Model offers transparent business practices and alignment of interests that are rarely found elsewhere.

Unsung Heroes

"If you look at the science and aren't pessimistic, you don't understand the data. But if you meet the people who are working to restore this earth, and you aren't optimistic, you haven't got a pulse."

—Paul Hawken

HAVING OUTLINED THE Cool Effect Model in the previous chapter, you know that picking great carbon projects is the core of our business. And having shared with you the story of Proyecto Mirador and its 19 years in Honduras, you understand that developing carbon projects, especially if one strives to reach the Top of the Pyramid, is an arduous task.

Project development and carbon certification involve more than just hard work and skill.

How do people do it? Why?

It is certainly not for money or fame. What makes these people, who could succeed at whatever they choose, drop everything to develop carbon projects?

In this chapter, we will introduce you to three exceptional entrepreneurs who have driven their projects to the Top of the Pyramid, including: an 85-year-old former journalist with the energy and passion of a

140

20-something; a former corporate executive with a genius for achieving climate scale in some of the poorest locales on Earth; and a former Ivy League banker who left Wall Street to help change the world in the peatland forests of Indonesia. They are all unsung heroes, inspired to help people and help save the planet.

Each of them possesses Cool Effect Leadership Values: Persistence, Integrity, Passion, and Aspirations. These qualities make all the difference. And while these terms defy simple definitions, you will know them when you see them in the following stories.

Dr. Arne Fjørtoft, CEO, Worldview International Foundation

Dr. Arne Fjørtoft began his career in the 1960s as a journalist in Norway, reporting on international matters, with a particular interest in sustainable development and human rights. He initiated his first sustainable development project in 1976, working with disadvantaged fishing communities in Sri Lanka, and founded Worldview International Foundation (WIF) in 1979.

WIF today focuses on blue carbon initiatives in Southeast Asia and Africa. Under Arne's leadership, WIF has planted over 75 million mangrove trees in coastal forests that sequester CO_2 from the atmosphere, protect coastlines, promote biodiversity, and provide food sources while helping local communities thrive sustainably.

Having worked with Arne since 2017, we find much to admire, including his persistence and dedication to his mission and a youthful exuberance and energy that belie his decades of good works. Arne says in the following story, "We will never give up planting trees of hope."

Arne Fjørtoft, CEO, Worldview International Foundation,
with Cool Effect Director of Research Sid Yadav.

The miracle tree

I became aware of mangrove trees after the deadly tsunami in Asia in 2004. The tsunami struck like an iron fist, killing 228,000 people and bringing devastation and hardship to millions in 14 countries. But in areas with mangrove forests, the communities were miraculously saved. This triggered me to study the wonder of life-saving mangrove protection.

In studying the mangroves further, it became crystal clear that restoring destroyed mangrove forests is the most cost-effective climate solution. Mangroves:

- Mitigate up to five times more CO_2 than terrestrial trees.

- Store 80% of carbon permanently in the soil, compared to 20% in the soil with terrestrial trees.

- Protect lives and homes from tsunamis, cyclones, and other extreme weather.

- Minimize shoreline erosion due to sea level rise.

- Build up the land with falling leaves and branches.

- Clean run-offs for the protection of the oceans.

- Increase coastal seafood resources by 50%.

- Provide life-bearing ecosystem services.

Nowhere else can we get all these stacked benefits delivered from nature. It has been widely proven that mangrove forests are the most efficient climate machines, working 24-7 in mitigating climate change. And the trees keep growing each season, blooming with flowers and creating seeds, multiplying new plants for a better future.

Unfortunately, these unassuming, strange trees with crooked root systems growing in salty water are being ravaged by careless human development. The yearly destruction of mangroves is estimated to add billions of tons of CO_2 to the atmosphere. Restoration can reverse that trend and help us to avert the worst calamities. It will also protect endangered species and foster biodiversity. The ultimate impact will come when more responsible people and companies take on the task of planting more trees. Mangrove forests are crying for help!

Initially, with minimal resources at WIF, our road to success was very steep climbing. The carbon market crashed in the wake of the Kyoto Protocol, and funding was scarce, if available at all. We had to lift ourselves up by the hair, mobilizing all available resources, determined never to give up.

Our situation changed dramatically when Cool Effect recognized WIF. Cool Effect provided enormous support by providing access to carbon credit financing and, just as important, by boosting our morale. Cool Effect gave us confidence that we could succeed in our mission.

With the private sector taking bolder steps in offsetting their carbon footprints, new funding in mangrove restoration became possible. The exploding interest in blue carbon has propelled us to the top of the high-quality chain. WIF was the first in 2022 to be awarded a triple AAA rating for successful mangrove restoration by BeZero, a carbon rating agency. In addition to mangroves, we have also gained valuable experience in seaweed production in cooperation with 90 communities in Myanmar and Thailand.

So far, WIF has planted 75 million trees, which will capture 46 million tons of CO_2 over 20 years. The target for 2023 is to plant 25 million trees, estimated to capture another 16 million tons. The total will be 100 million trees mitigating 62 million tons, more than the entire annual emissions of Norway. This self-sustaining wonder of nature never fails. Technical solutions are less effective and extremely costly. Nothing can compete with nature, but the world is losing nature at an alarming rate.

We strongly believe in the miracle tree and the miracle of cooperation across borders. In 2022, WIF expanded mangrove restoration to Gambia, Sierra Leone, and Tanzania in Africa, and to Sri Lanka, Malaysia, Papua New Guinea, and Indonesia in Asia.

We will never give up planting trees of hope.

Sandeep Roy Choudhury, Co-Founder, VNV Advisory Services

Sandeep is CEO and Co-Founder at VNV Advisory Services, a social enterprise that works in rural communities on challenges related to climate change in South and Southeast Asia. VNV's low-carbon projects include sustainable agriculture, social forestry, coastal resilience, clean cooking, clean air, drinking water, rural energy access, and waste management.

Sandeep's ability to deliver funding where it is most needed, efficiently and timely, makes him a rock star in the world's poorest places. He is a charismatic leader, and people love him wherever he goes; but more importantly, he builds livelihoods while building emission-reducing projects.

Sandeep tells his remarkable and moving story in the following.

Sandeep Roy Choudhury, Co-Founder, VNV Advisory Services.

I was born and raised in the foothills of the Himalayas, an early life that was slow yet meaningful, one with nature and time. Later, work life in the cities was not so meaningful, and utterly disillusioning. The corporate race, seeing the world around me unraveling, led me to leave to focus on going back to my early life ideas, albeit with a lot more business in me now. A business of the ethical kind, I hoped. The idea was to work with the communities most impacted by climate change.

Scale is of the essence

The massive nature of climate change adaptation required in the Global South is unprecedented and unfathomable. Scale is of the essence. The solutions need to be big and scalable. In the beginning, it was so challenging to raise money for projects. It became clear that to succeed, the financing system for carbon had to change. There had to be a business case for climate projects.

Then came carbon credits and the Voluntary Carbon Market. Carbon credits connect small, grass-root community organizations in the Global South with companies and individuals in the developed world who take responsibility for their emissions. For a social enterprise like ours, the carbon market was a transformative breakthrough. Suddenly, with access to capital, so many important projects became possible. We had villages to electrify, drinking water to provide, and kitchens to retrofit in rural households with biogas as cooking fuel.

To speed up project implementation, we partner with project developers already working in local communities, in some cases for as long as 30 years, but who needed help to succeed and grow. Their local knowledge, and the trust and goodwill they have earned with the local people, are invaluable. Today we work in a partnership network of over 150 such organizations. This has helped us scale immensely.

For example, one inspirational gentleman in Bangladesh, Dr. Khaleq, ran the most impressive clean cooking program I had ever seen. He had 200 people working for him and another 1,000 independent entrepreneurs who made the cookstoves. But in 2013, his sources of finance dried up. All 1,300 people were at risk of losing their jobs, and Dr. Khaleq's dream to provide cookstoves across Bangladesh seemed to end.

But in 2014, we started working closely with Dr. Khaleq to raise money, little by little, by selling carbon credit to companies across the U.S., Europe, and East Asia. Today, the project directly employs more than 1,500 people, with another 7,000 entrepreneurs building stoves. This same organization can now work on clean water access, sustainable agriculture, agri-forestry, mangrove reforestation, disaster management, and various other projects. This is what transformation looks like at scale. The Voluntary Carbon Market makes all this possible.

Grateful

I share dreams with people of impeccable integrity, who are gritty, and determined to achieve the unachievable—inspirational people who share my ideas of scale. I am also privileged to work with some of the finest people on earth, but who are also some of the most needy and deserving.

- In Bangladesh among the refugee Rohingya communities, 800,000 women, children, and helpless families.

- In Myanmar, where communities are ravaged by a bloody coup and rural folk have no livelihoods.

- In Himalayan Nepal, a place of pristine beauty but ravaged by flash floods every year and one of the most vulnerable regions in the world.

- In vast and populous India, where smallholder farming communities struggle with prolonged drought.

- In Indonesia, with some of the loveliest people on earth, where coastal communities fight a losing battle against climate change.

- In the landlocked paradise of Laos, where poverty is at unprecedented levels, and yet the people carry on with a smile every day.

- In Timor-Leste, another country at the mercy of the elements, where people fight for basic livelihoods.

- In the coastal communities of Madagascar, where people live without water, without electricity, without schools, without toilets.

- In Ghana, known for chocolate but not so much for the plight of the growers and smallholders. They are the backbone of the small but growing economy, struggling to make ends meet.

My job allows me to work with these people. Grateful.

Millions of people are thrown into abject poverty every day as the climate changes. We owe it to them, to the people who fight this fight every day. These people deserve respect and recognition. They are fighting a battle not of their own creation.

My organization VNV today is engaged with low-carbon projects helping over three million small farmers, over seven million rural households, and over two million people in indigenous forest communities. The Voluntary Carbon Market has helped to make this possible.

Grateful.

Dharsono Hartono, CEO, Katingan Mentaya Project

When Cool Effect heard about Indonesia's Katingan Mentaya peatlands preservation project, we immediately wanted to know more.

Peatlands comprise just 3% of the Earth's land surface but store more carbon than all other vegetation combined. The problem is that the destruction of peatlands for commercial use accounts for almost 5% of global CO_2 emissions. The Katingan Mentaya project protects and preserves a massive Indonesian peatland forest, avoiding 7.5 million tonnes of carbon emissions annually.

That is an amazing accomplishment. How was it achieved?

Better to let Dharsono Hartono, CEO of the Katingan Mentaya project, tell the story himself.

Dharsono Hartono, CEO, Katingan Mentaya Project.

I grew up in Indonesia, received my undergraduate and graduate degrees at Cornell, and worked as a banker in New York. When I returned to Indonesia in 2007, I met my friend and classmate Rezal Kusumaatmadja, who believed carbon credits offered a market-based opportunity to save the environment and help local people. I was skeptical, but he persisted and eventually convinced me that managing climate projects as a business could be a game changer for the world.

"When it comes from the heart, you can accomplish anything."

We started looking into peatlands because they store so much carbon. We heard about an area with over 150,000 hectares of forested peatlands in Central Kalimantan, which the government had planned to convert into pulp and paper plantations. That's more than twice the size of Singapore. Luckily for us and the planet, the plan was never enacted. The opportunity for us was that, in Indonesia, one could apply for a concession to manage public land. We were two young men with a dream, so we applied.

The problem was that an environmental concession was a new idea at that time. The government agents didn't understand and were slow to review our proposal. To keep things moving, I would wait at the government offices all day, pestering people to make sure that our application was getting attention. I think they finally approved our application just to get rid of me! But it took us six years to get the approval.

Six years. I was in my 30s, in the prime of my working years, and if I failed... My wife always supported my dream, but sometimes I thought I should cut my losses. I had a family. I could get a regular job.

One time, when I was having doubts, I visited one of the local villages in Kalimantan and took a ferry across the river. There was a young girl on the ferry on her way to school. The boatman didn't charge the young girl the crossing fare when we reached the other side. He explained, "The girl is going to school. We should not charge people if they want to go to school." I was so impressed with that vision. I thought, "It is not just for the climate. It is also for these good people and this beautiful place. I need to do this." I returned to my wife and said, "I'll give it another year."

We got the approval. The rest is history. I truly believe that you can accomplish anything when it comes from the heart.

The lens of awe

Managing climate projects has also made me realize that we must think differently about how we value businesses. Business valuation has for so long been stuck in the simple metrics of ROE, ROI, IRR, and P/E ratios. That's business seen through the lens of finance, and while those principles are useful, they are incomplete, far too narrow, and have allowed us to damage our planet. We need to change that. We need to recognize that people everywhere have value; nature and biodiversity have value. We must measure positive and negative business impacts across a broader spectrum.

We cannot think just about extraction and ownership and profit. We have to think like stewards. We are stewards of each other, the planet, and the future. When we do that, we see value not just through the lens of finance, but through the lens of awe. The world economy has to be, first and foremost, about people and the planet, including the well-being of disadvantaged communities. This is not just some utopian pipe dream. Because of carbon financing, these things are possible now.

I want to pay it forward to show the world that this is a journey for humanity. It is not just about carbon credits; it is way beyond that. So much can be accomplished. Our mission is to inspire and empower a new generation of leaders and changemakers to attain a more sustainable, equitable world.

Don't give up. We are finally getting this right.

These are all exceptional people, and their projects are outstanding. Each of the projects embraces superior business models, has reached the Top of the Pyramid, employs global best practices, commits to the long term, and is driven by leadership values. For these reasons, each of the projects has benefitted by being able to source funding through the Voluntary Carbon Market. They represent the VCM at its best and, if many more follow their example, the VCM's best hope for the future.

Dream Fulfilled

"With the idea of the butterfly effect, we are thousands of tiny individuals. But if you and I and 10,000 others like us come together, we start to really get some attention."

—Dee Lawrence, Co-Founder, Cool Effect

B Y 2 0 2 3, Cool Effect had come a long way since Dee and I agreed to establish it over a glass of wine. After a six-year start-up period, there was a bright light at the end of the long tunnel as we finally fulfilled our mission of supporting high-integrity projects and allocating capital to disadvantaged communities in the Global South. Cool Effect did not need to pivot again, but only to execute the Cool Effect Model.

Great customers acknowledged that only high-quality projects should be included in the VCM, and Cool Effect was recognized as a valuable partner in selecting high-integrity carbon credits. While we had saved Cool Effect, the question remained if we could also help the VCM become committed to high-integrity carbon credits.

Despite the ten-year bear market in carbon, which finally ended in 2021, Cool Effect has achieved more than we might have hoped for, assisting over 3,200 businesses to purchase credits to offset their emissions, generating funding for carbon projects in excess of $47 million, and reducing carbon emissions by 6.4 million tonnes.

We need a Milky Way

While we are pleased with Cool Effect's contribution to the fight against climate change, we know that far more will be required from all of us; far more than Cool Effect alone could accomplish. Think of it this way: all companies now actively offsetting their emissions with the carbon credits of so many great carbon projects are a few bright stars in the sky. What we need is a Milky Way of thousands of such stars. That's where the Voluntary Carbon Market comes in.

And we need wisdom

The potential of the VCM is enormous. It is an essential component in the fight against climate change. But the VCM is still very young, in the earliest stage of development, and risks abound. We must get this right. There is no room for failure. We all want to be hopeful about the VCM, but we must also be wise.

In Part Four, we discuss the future of the VCM.

Cool Effect
Photo Well

Permian Global and Rimba Makmur Utama, Katingan Mentaya Project,
Central Kalimantan, Indonesia.

The project protects 149,800 hectares of a peat swamp ecosystem. The project
has established seven socioeconomic zones to coordinate the application of
funds from the sale of carbon within surrounding communities.

The Katingan Mentaya project supports farmers by supplying seeds and then finding a market for resulting produce such as this galangal.

The Katingan Mentaya project area is surrounded by water.

Worldview International, Reforestation and restoration of degraded mangroves, Myanmar.

Village members planting mangrove seedlings in a Myanmar coastal area.

Healthy mangroves support a regeneration of the local wildlife in coastal Myanmar.

VNV Advisory Services, developing climate resilience of the coastal communities of Sundarbans through mangrove afforestation, Southeast India.

Mangrove seedlings are transported by boat to the mangrove planting site, unloaded by hand and taken to the village work team.

Local village work team participating in the first planting of 6.5 million mangroves on an island in the Sundarbans.

157

A local village resident holding a native mangrove
species for planting in the Sundarbans.

A family of Royal Bengal Tigers in the wilds of the reserve close
to the Sundarbans mangrove planting project. Mangroves are a
favorite habitat for the endangered tigers.

Boomitra, Carbon Farming in the Indo-Gangetic Plains, northwest of Delhi, India.

Traditional burning of rice stubble in the fields depletes soil of nutrients and causes enormous air pollution during harvest time.

Harvesting rice in India is a labor intensive job. Here rice sheaves are banged against an oil drum to release the rice grains. The remaining stalk is used for mulch, electricity generation, or feeding cattle.

The "Happy Seeder" machine, made available with project
resources, provides an alternative to burning rice crop residue.
It chops rice stubble, turns it under and plants the next crop,
saving time, water, and preserving carbon in the soil.

Dee Lawrence and members of a women's cooperative that works
closely with the project.

PART FOUR

The Voluntary Carbon Market

A Framework
for the VCM

"We need every tool available working at full speed to channel investment toward keeping the global temperature within 1.5°C. A transparent, liquid, high-integrity voluntary carbon market is one very important tool we can use to achieve that goal."

—Annette Nazareth, Co-Chair, IC VCM; former SEC Commissioner

Where we've been

THROUGHOUT OUR JOURNEY in this book, we have traversed all the components of the carbon credit supply chain. We introduced projects and their leaders, like Doña Emilia and Pak Dharsono, who are delivering real emission reductions in incredibly challenging conditions. We have discussed how the Standards—the voluntary governance organizations such as Gold Standard and Verra—constantly strive to improve their methodologies to keep up with the rapid advancement of cutting-edge carbon science, policy, and on-the-ground conditions.

We have learned about Cool Effect's embrace of global best practices and transparent business practices. We have heard the voices of sustainability executives, like Lisa Shibata and Patrick Flynn, who have told us that leading corporations can only achieve Net Zero by 2050 with a fully functioning VCM. We have seen the VCM direct billions of dollars of capital to disadvantaged communities in the Global South and beyond.

These voices focus on defining high-quality carbon credits, rigorous methodologies, and global best practices. Their stories provide us with the hope that the VCM can accelerate change for corporations, directing mitigation capital into the most impactful and cost-effective parts of the ecosystem.

Where we are going

"High-integrity Voluntary Carbon Markets have the potential to help deliver local benefits to frontline communities and lessen the burden of climate change. Done well, they can also provide a blueprint for carbon pricing on a global scale to accelerate the global climate transition."

—Sonia Medina, Executive Director—Climate,
Children's Investment Fund Foundation

The size of the Voluntary Carbon Market reached $2 billion in 2021, four times its size in 2020. That is impressive, and it is good news, but it is a tiny fraction of the scale it needs to reach. To achieve its potential, the VCM must become a viable asset class in global financial markets, and we have work to do to get there.

Financial markets are built on information—information that is abundant, reliable and standardized. For the VCM to become an asset class in global financial markets, greater transparency and consistency of information are required so that carbon projects can be reliably analyzed, competitively compared, and correctly valued based on quality. To achieve this efficiency, current weaknesses in the VCM must be rectified.

Climate change needs all the tools
in the toolbox

Climate change is a very tough problem. It advances with certainty yet goes mostly unnoticed in our day-to-day lives until CNN reports that a hurricane destroyed a coastal community, fires burned remote villages, or heatwaves caused us to buy air conditioners for our homes that we never needed before. Climate change is like compound interest. We did not notice the shift for many years, but it accumulated at a surprising rate as hurricanes, heat waves, and other climate events become more frequent and disruptive.

In 1977, Exxon's own scientists raised the flag of "catastrophic consequences" from rising CO_2 concentrations in the atmosphere. At that time, CO_2 concentrations were 320 parts per million (ppm). Today, CO_2 concentrations are 420 ppm. Note also that over the last decade, the carbon concentration in the atmosphere has further increased despite less economic activity during Covid, and despite early efforts on the part of many to reduce emissions. CO_2 accumulation in the atmosphere over the last decade only highlights how tough it is to reduce emissions at a time when declines are required. It feels like we are trying to stop a train without brakes.

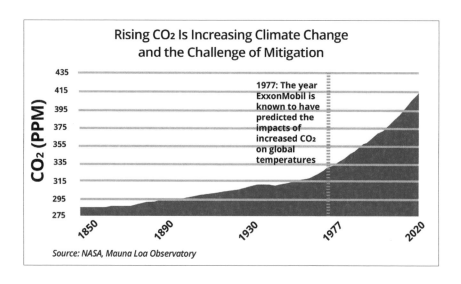

And there is an added challenge that increases the urgency to reverse emissions growth. During that same period, from 1977 to 2022, global inflation compounded at 5.68% per annum. So, not only have the CO_2 concentrations in the atmosphere become larger with time, but the price tag for all types of adaptation and mitigation has become astronomically higher for an already indebted global society.

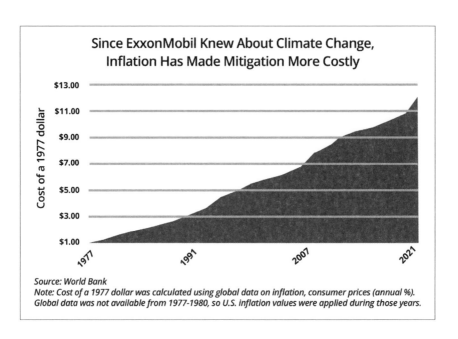

Since ExxonMobil Knew About Climate Change, Inflation Has Made Mitigation More Costly

Source: World Bank
Note: Cost of a 1977 dollar was calculated using global data on inflation, consumer prices (annual %). Global data was not available from 1977-1980, so U.S. inflation values were applied during those years.

Climate change, in terms of both its severity and the cost of mitigation, is worsening. The frequency of extreme weather events is now growing faster than the increase of CO_2 in the atmosphere. If we continue to muddle ahead in our response to climate change, science points to a dangerous future. The following chart shows a very dangerous trend: occurrences of extreme weather increase even faster than averages.

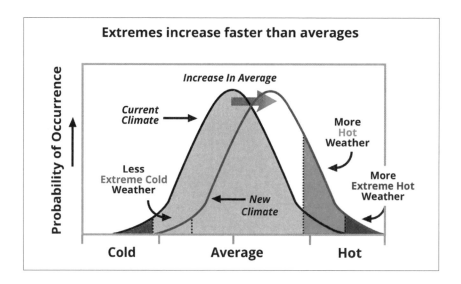

All of this means that we need to act immediately and utilize all the tools in our toolbox. We must pursue even the wildest climate change technologies as they might prove to be a valuable tool in this fight.

One of the essential tools the world already has in our toolbox is the Voluntary Carbon Market.

The VCM Is an Essential Tool

"There's not a company on Earth that I am aware of that has control over all of its emissions sources and certainty on how to decarbonize all of their operations. This means that carbon credit markets have to be a part of companies' Net Zero transition strategies. High-integrity market-based systems are essential to an orderly and affordable transition to Net Zero and to ambitious near-term climate action."

—Alexia Kelly, Managing Director, Carbon Policy & Markets Initiative, High Tide Foundation; former Netflix sustainability executive

THE VCM IS not *the* solution; it is *a* solution. The VCM fits into the vast portfolio of actions the world needs to take. The VCM is not a substitute for reducing operational emissions at their source. As Patrick Flynn told us earlier in the book, the role of carbon credits in climate strategy is "last but not later." Operational reductions must always be the priority for corporations.

However, as corporates struggle to decarbonize, high-integrity carbon credits are a means to offset emissions effectively and immediately. The VCM can deliver essential benefits to corporations and society:

• It puts a price on carbon to communicate the cost of climate emissions—

168

an essential element of integrating the true costs of climate pollution into the global economy.

- It enables corporates to immediately complement their efforts to reduce their operational reductions of carbon emissions, increasing their ambition and impact.

- It is a market mechanism that can advance essential ecosystem restoration, support critical biodiversity, reduce air pollution, increase climate resilience and improve social outcomes for disadvantaged communities, particularly in the Global South.

- It is a platform to mobilize billions of dollars of private capital into projects that reduce carbon emissions and accelerate the energy transition that would otherwise not have occurred.

It has been said that climate change is the ultimate global problem and that carbon emission reduction projects are the ultimate local solution to climate change. Connecting the two is the promise of the Voluntary Carbon Market. However, the VCM needs to create a compelling and robust governance framework to fulfill that promise.

In our politicized world, where even closing unhealthy leaks of gas from our stoves is seen as a threat to the fossil fuel industry, it should not be a surprise that the VCM attracts much criticism, and not all of it constructive.

The Age of Discovery

The value of constructive criticism

THE VCM FACES daily attacks from the media and the Ivory Tower academics who doubt its ability to deliver real emission reductions. At times, the attacks focus on individual projects; at other times, critics attempt to take down whole sectors, such as the cookstove or forestry industry. At other times, commentators just seem to want headlines.

As we know, it is easy to criticize actions of the past through the lens of today, and to deny that the methodologies and science have advanced significantly since 2010. Such criticism is blind to the value of the VCM and its essential role.

On the other hand, there is also substantial constructive criticism—insightful criticism coupled with suggested remedies—which creates value in the VCM. We must recognize that the VCM is in an Age of Discovery; a time when those in the market need to acknowledge weaknesses and work prudently to create an enduring framework for the future. Criticism is an important component of the Age of Discovery. It helps differentiate between projects, methodologies, intermediaries, and buyers that are on Top of the Pyramid and those that are not.

All participants acknowledge the structural challenges of the VCM's current patchwork regulations:

- Governance of the VCM is scattered across a balkanized group of small non-profit organizations that approve methodologies for calculating the impact of a given carbon project. The Standards must seek to develop applicable methodologies on a global level that account for permutations of project circumstances while keeping up with fast-advancing science and technology.

- Methodologies lag scientific advancements and the implementation of new policies and regulations. This makes it incredibly easy for the media to point fingers at weaknesses. The following chart shows a simple visualization of the lag between methodologies and science and what we call the Period of Criticism, when methodologies lag the science. As shown in the graph, the Period of Criticism will shrink over time as technologies and methodologies converge to near real-time calculations of emission reductions.

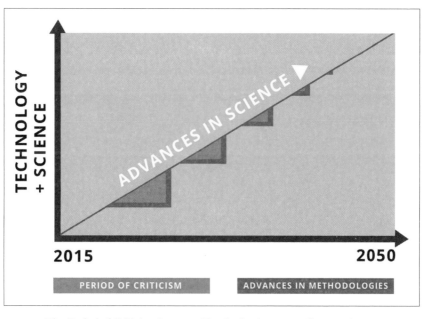

The Period of Criticism is caused by the lag between climate science and carbon measurement methodologies.

- The trading of carbon credits has limited barriers to entry, and negligible regulatory capital requirements or legislated best practices, leading to unscrupulous intermediaries operating in the market. Unregulated markets bring undisclosed markups, proprietary trading, and hidden fees that unsuspecting developers, disadvantaged communities, and buyers inevitably pay.

- Corporate buyers exaggerate emission reduction claims that amount to greenwashing due to the limited ability of stakeholders to hold management accountable. This leaves well-intentioned corporates increasingly hesitant to disclose carbon credit purchases for fear of a backlash in the media, a practice that has become known as "greenhushing."

These structural weaknesses of the VCM can be rectified by improving the governance and regulation of the VCM. Failure is not an option, nor is strengthening the VCM framework impossible. But the framework should be created with a market-based solution in mind. The alternative is to let heavy-handed politicians try to do it.

Government: a Bottom of the Pyramid solution

Suppose for a moment that critics and naysayers successfully block efforts to create a robust VCM architecture. In that case, governments worldwide will be forced by the increase of CO_2 concentrations in the atmosphere to intervene directly to reduce carbon emissions. That's an easy option for governments to embrace, but it is an inefficient option. Government intervention will likely come in the form of a plethora of carbon taxes on individuals and corporations that raise issues:

- How will countries with differing political views on climate change agree on implementing a global carbon tax system, given each country's narrow self-interest?

- Could we avoid an overabundance of border carbon tax adjustments that would cause mayhem in global trade, at a time when deglobalization is already on the rise?

- Can governments allocate capital more efficiently than a market-based VCM?

- Would governments directly tax carbon credits, or include credits as part of their obligation under the Paris Agreement, thereby disincentivizing new projects and crowding out market growth?

- Could governments understand the concept of Top of the Pyramid projects?

Without an integrated global governance system, a government-imposed set of carbon taxes would lead to a slower delivery of climate solutions at scale, less economic efficiency, black market trading in goods, and higher global inflation. In short, a government-led carbon tax could lead to a decade of delay in climate mitigation.

Water off a duck's back

The growing pains and criticisms faced by the VCM in our Age of Discovery are not unique to this market. The history of stock markets worldwide provides an excellent comparison to the VCM of today. The early stages of a market's development are always when high-profile failures occur, and a governance framework is created to flush out the bottom-of-the-pyramid actors.

Stock analysts, investors, reporters, and short sellers play a vital role in identifying strong performers and flushing out weak ones, and the VCM is going through the same process now. Stock markets offer examples where improved transparency, analysis, and governance eventually turned companies and industries into large and productive engines of global growth.

Thankfully, the VCM Framework is being created when the market is $2 billion in size, unlike the cryptocurrency industry, which hit a wall at $3 trillion. With the benefit of hindsight, the crypto industry might have considered adopting a framework like Top of Pyramid behavior before it reached $3 trillion in market size and subjected investors to massive losses.

Leaders within the VCM simply need to maintain their confidence and push full speed ahead. And in the following chapter we propose an agenda for success to guide us forward.

An Agenda for Success

"Regulators need to require full disclosure of climate risk— which includes not just physical dangers but also direct and indirect financial risks."

—Joseph Stiglitz, Nobel Prize-winning economist

WE STATED EARLIER that the VCM needs to scale to realize its full potential. And to achieve that scale, the VCM must become a viable asset class in global financial markets.

Allow us to expand upon a maxim of the financial markets:

Transparency leads to Trust;

Trust leads to Scale;

and with Scale, the VCM becomes a financial asset class.

What actions do we need to take now to achieve this?

- All components of the VCM supply chain must work toward improved disclosure: developers, the Standards and their methodologies, market intermediaries, and buyers. We need more disclosure at all levels, and we need it urgently. Only with better disclosure can we judge the integrity of participants. Who aspires to reach the upper parts of the pyramid, and who does not?

- In partnership with governments, regulators must create an environment where Top of the Pyramid participants reap the greatest rewards from market-based incentives.

- There are many components to how the market can reward the best and flush the worst. These include institutionalizing global best practices into a rules-based infrastructure, investing in the professionalism of the industry, valuing carbon emission reductions along with social benefits in the Global South, and boosting transparency of the price signals.

- We must turn high-integrity carbon credits into a new financial asset class. Much climate mitigation capital can be mobilized by engaging Wall Street. ESG investing and Net Zero commitments have vastly increased the potential market for high-quality environmental assets. Carbon credits fit nicely into this category. Wall Street needs the VCM to create a market-based system with price signals and rewards, and then Wall Street will do what it does best: mobilize capital.

- We must address weaknesses within the VCM that often act as speed bumps to outsiders and provide fuel to critics. We need ever-stronger methodologies, transaction transparency, and a cohort of project analysts who can evaluate the management and finances of projects and market intermediaries. And we need to resolve many of the arcane and confusing rabbit holes that inhibit investment, like uncertainty over Article 6 of the Paris Agreement Share of Proceeds taxes, taxes on the export of credits, and non-additional jurisdictional REDD+ projects. We must get on with the business of flushing the toilet on bad players and bad ideas at all levels.

- We must institutionalize rules to reward participants who bring passion, integrity, persistence, and aspiration to their daily work. A vast world of future leaders is waiting to engage in the storied task of slowing the trajectory of climate change. Climate change is not a short-term fight. We need to incentivize dedicated leaders committed to ambitious growth over the long term.

As the VCM moves into its next stage of expansion, we must implement a governance architecture for the next several decades to ensure that failure does not happen. Thankfully, there are ongoing efforts worldwide to create such a framework. Help is on the way.

Help Is on the Way

"Hope is not a strategy."

—Alexia Kelly, Managing Director, Carbon Policy & Markets Initiative, High Tide Foundation; former Netflix sustainability executive

A SIGNIFICANT AMOUNT OF work is already underway today to create the VCM Framework for the next decade. It is happening across all sectors, from projects to buyers of carbon credits.

To build trust, these global efforts must improve methodologies, governance, business practices, and transparency. The VCM must create appropriate incentives and allow the power of the market economy to build scale rapidly. This VCM Framework must eventually be passed to government regulators to institutionalize the rules.

Advancement of the VCM Framework is essential for the carbon credit asset class to operate as an effective tool for corporate buyers with high ambition. This joint effort to structure the VCM Framework includes participation from non-profits, regulators, corporations, standards, lawyers, bankers, developers, scientists, rating agencies, academics, and market intermediaries. Everyone has a hand in creating the consensus, and all stakeholders will be required to implement the unique and comprehensive VCM Framework.

The key principles of the VCM Framework

Progress is evident across the VCM supply chain, focusing on governance, science and technology, standards, global best practices, and an appropriate role for government oversight. The future Top of the Pyramid VCM governance system will be based on the following pillars:

- Strong Governance and High Transparency

- State of the Art Science and Technology

- Top of the Pyramid Projects and Methodologies

- Top of the Pyramid Buyers

Below, we hear the voices of some of the leaders in the field who are striving to create a VCM Framework for the next two decades.

Strong Governance and High Transparency

Integrity Council for the Voluntary Carbon Market (IC VCM)

The IC VCM is an independent governance body for the Voluntary Carbon Market. Its mission is to ensure credit integrity in the Voluntary Carbon Market. The IC VCM aims to set and enforce a global benchmark for high-integrity carbon credits with rigorous thresholds on disclosure and sustainable development. It aims to ensure a unified, global set of rules to indicate Top of the Pyramid governance organizations and credit categories.

> *"At the Integrity Council, our goal is to build a high-integrity, transparent voluntary market. The most effective way to achieve this is within a supportive policy environment that promotes high integrity across the whole market, including the supply, trading and use of credits.*

"This means the private and public sector working in collaboration to design and promote effective frameworks that drive ambition and continual improvement, and inform decision-making so the market is more efficient at allocating capital to the most impactful solutions."

—Annette Nazareth, Co-Chair, IC VCM; former SEC Commissioner

State of the Art Science and Technology

Science and technology are rapidly advancing in all areas of carbon mitigation, improving both the effectiveness of carbon projects and the measurement, monitoring, and verification of carbon reductions.

"Data collected from space has created new metrics for measuring our changing Earth. Planet Labs is at the forefront, advancing satellite technology and building the earth data infrastructure that will enable us to empirically measure carbon stored in forests and other ecosystems, emissions rates, the health of water, and biodiversity. This data will greatly accelerate the accurate calculation of sustainable and regenerative land use to allow humans to be in right relationship with nature."

—Robbie Schingler, Co-Founder of Planet Labs, which operates a system of satellites that circle the globe on a continuous basis, providing us data required for a more regenerative economy and a sustainable planet.

"We need a global, state-of-the-art accounting system to measure and monitor emission reduction efforts and to provide definitive and actionable information to policymakers and carbon market actors. Technology and data from providers like Planet Labs are the linchpin of this accounting system. Remote sensing techniques are mature enough to allow near-real-time monitoring of land use activities such as deforestation and carbon emissions. Integrating a wide range of remote sensing

observations in verifiable carbon standards and methodologies will ultimately build trust in carbon markets worldwide."

—Sassan Saatchi, a senior research scientist at the NASA Jet Propulsion Laboratory and the CEO of C-Trees.org, a non-profit satellite data analytics company focused on forest carbon. Sassan takes the remote sensing data from a variety of air and space sources and performs specialized modeling and ground-truthing to increase the accuracy of measuring emission savings from forests.

"Leaders such as Robbie Schingler, working with cutting-edge scientists like Sassan Saatchi, will help the world identify Top of Pyramid carbon reduction projects and steer the VCM toward a position of high integrity. Science and technology, and the great minds behind them, are our key to unlocking the potential of a sustainable economy. We need to roll up our sleeves and do the work. Hope is not a strategy."

—Alexia Kelly, Managing Director, Carbon Policy & Markets Initiative, High Tide Foundation; former Netflix sustainability executive.

Top of the Pyramid Projects and Methodologies

The Gold Standard, VERRA, and other standards which verify carbon reductions and certify carbon credits, are placing increased demands on project developers for greater transparency.

"What we are seeing today is the natural result of the continuing maturity of a market experiencing enormous growth. Two decades ago, no one thought the Voluntary Carbon Market would be in the leadership role it is in today, but something happened—when sky-high plans for government action failed to materialize, the VCM is what worked: millions of dollars delivered real impacts for the climate and communities.

"As the world's leading standard-setting body for the Voluntary Carbon Market, Verra has certified over 2,000 projects around the world that have reduced or removed over 1.1 billion tons

of GHG emissions. That is just the start of what we need to do, but it is real progress and real impact in a sea of failed schemes and faded hopes. And as the need for action only grows more urgent, we think it has important lessons and points the way to a livable future."

—David Antonioli, Former CEO of Verra

Top of the Pyramid Buyers

Voluntary Carbon Markets Integrity Initiative (VCMI)

The VCMI is developing a Claims Code of Practice that will guide companies to make transparent and credible claims about their progress toward a longer-term Net Zero commitment.

"A critical component of the VCM is creating an institutional framework that permits companies to make accurate claims about their climate actions while at the same time protecting against corporations' overstatement of their actions."

—Mark Kenber, Executive Director, VCMI

Government support at the Top of the Pyramid

There is an enormous difference between government oversight of the VCM and direct government intervention in global markets. If the VCM Framework can be implemented widely across the globe, the VCM does not require government intervention but rather government oversight to ensure that the Framework is implemented fairly and openly.

Listed below are some of the actions that governments around the world can take to embrace the Framework and drive growth and quality of the VCM:

- Support the VCM as a market-based solution that supports broader climate change mitigation goals.

- Push for increased transparency. We need legislated disclosure over the use of proceeds of carbon revenue. What is the split of the carbon revenue between the market intermediary, the project developer, and the local communities? What should a project developer or market intermediary receive as compensation? This area is wide open to abuse, and the only way to resolve it is with more transparency.

- Create the transaction infrastructure that will require disclosure on pricing and markups by market intermediaries.

- Embrace advances in science and technology in line with the understanding that there is no silver bullet in climate change.

- Support and legally enforce the VCM Framework, in much the same way as the Securities and Exchange Commission regulates the U.S. securities markets.

Putting these principles in place within a new architecture will allow the VCM to scale to a size not previously imagined.

The VCM Comes of Age

"The 2008 financial crisis showed what can happen when even a small part of the world's asset base (U.S. subprime mortgages) gets repriced. The repricing of assets that are likely to be affected by climate change could have systemic effects that will dwarf those of 2008. The fossil-fuel sector is just the tip of the (melting) iceberg."

—Joseph Stiglitz, Nobel Prize-winning economist

N EW ENTRANTS, UNDERSTANDING the urgent need to take action on climate change, are bringing new pools of capital and expertise to the VCM. Growth is already underway even while the VCM Framework is being modernized.

This chapter highlights how leading groups see the VCM as an essential market.

To mention a few of the advancements we are witnessing:

- Corporations increasingly recognize high-integrity carbon credits as necessary to meet their Net Zero commitments.

- Corporations are investing in projects in exchange for a fixed stream of carbon credits in the future rather than buying credits on the spot market.

- Venture capital, private equity, investment banks, and institutional capital are entering the market for the first time, searching for high-integrity credits and cash returns.

- Rating agencies and market intermediaries are adding sophistication to project analysis.

The participants' growth has highlighted the industry's need to develop solid research skills to analyze the wide range of projects involved in the VCM.

Again, the needs of the VCM have a parallel to the financial markets. Like stock-picking in the stock market, selection of Top of Pyramid projects requires a high degree of professionalism. Just as stock picking entails analysts poring over financial statements to gain investment insights, future project pickers within the carbon market will need a whole host of unique analysis skills to select Top of the Pyramid projects.

In many ways, project picking is more complicated than the analysis of company financial statements. And for the VCM to achieve the level of success, the professionalism of participants needs to increase.

Project analysis becomes a profession

The MBA and CFA programs provide well-established paths to a career in stock picking, and the VCM needs similar human resource development programs. The planet needs a Chartered Carbon Analyst (CCA) program modeled on the CFA program to arm the project-pickers of the future with the requisite analytical skills. And we need leading universities to create sophisticated sustainability programs—perhaps a master's degree in Project Analysis. Surely, these careers will be satisfying and incredibly thought-provoking.

Just as Wall Street analysts carry out company analysis, the CCA project-pickers of the future will be required to visit the projects, read the project documentation, think about the quality of management, understand the use of carbon credit proceeds, comprehend the complex carbon accounting principles, and consider how to value the return on investment after including values for the social benefits.

As the professionalism of project analysts in the VCM increases, confidence in the market will grow, encouraging more projects, financial intermediaries, and corporations to participate. As more entities enter the market, more voices will be heard, more projects will be competitively compared, and the market improvements will accelerate. This will allow the market to scale beyond what is currently contemplated at the higher end of the pyramid.

Carbon achieves scale as a financial asset class

New and innovative capital management strategies are already under development for institutional capital to enter the market, alongside impact and government investors. These funds are testing, with success, blending public and private capital to deliver environmental outcomes alongside risk-adjusted returns. A number of funds have been launched and closed, with successful returns delivered back to their investors, with more on the way.

Imagine for a second, in 2025: a major investment bank announces the creation of Carbon Fund 1, a $400 million entity funded by 20 corporate investors. The fund is managed by five recent Chartered Carbon Analyst program graduates. The fund's objective is to provide $20 million of capital to each of the 20 Top of the Pyramid projects in exchange for a stream of high-integrity carbon credits over 15 or 20 years. These credits will effectively be dividends corporations use to meet their Net Zero commitments.

The fund will give the buyers a stream of credits at a fixed price, thus locking in costs for an extended period. The syndication will reduce the volatility of the carbon credits through diversification. If one project fails to deliver its full carbon reductions, the margin of safety in the other 19 projects will likely cover the shortfall. This will vastly diminish the risk of public criticism.

Wouldn't other major investment banks have to follow suit to compete in the growing market with even larger syndications? Suppose an institutional investor with a Net Zero commitment buys an interest in the carbon fund to reduce its Scope 3 emissions. Wouldn't the institutional investor have a fiduciary obligation and a financial interest to pressure corporations to reduce their operational emissions? And if Mirador or Katingan is one of the projects elected, wouldn't more fuel-efficient cookstoves be built across Central America, or peatlands be protected in Indonesia?

When Wall Street investment banks begin to syndicate carbon funds, they will bring the financial markets' professionalism, transparency, regulations, and liquidity to the VCM. That is what they do. It is how Wall Street operates. And that is what we all want for the VCM.

As corporations and investors enter the VCM at a high level, opportunities open for Inverting the Pyramid, which is discussed in the final chapter.

Let's Invert the Pyramid and Change the World

"We are the first generation to feel the impact of climate change and the last generation that can do something about it."

—Former U.S. President Barack Obama

T HROUGHOUT THIS BOOK, we have heard from many of the unsung heroes on the front lines of climate change, from Honduras to India to Indonesia, to San Francisco to Hood River, Oregon. We learned of their efforts to deliver real additional emission reductions, create capital and jobs for impoverished communities, and accelerate the clean energy transition.

We have learned from sustainability officers at leading corporations that businesses cannot reach their Net Zero targets without carbon credits and are only interested in high-integrity credits.

We have learned from entities like the IC VCM and VCMI of the ongoing efforts to construct a durable Framework for the VCM to benefit all participants and the planet.

We have seen increasing interest from investment funds in carbon credits and imagined a near future where the VCM may become an asset class on Wall Street and in financial markets worldwide.

These leaders share a common sense of urgency over the impact of climate change on the globe. These are the voices of builders, not destroyers. They all aspire to reach the Top of the Pyramid.

As we successfully build the VCM Framework, the goal of the carbon market will be realized. All Top of the Pyramid players will grow, and the bottom-of-the-pyramid players will be flushed. This will allow us to Invert the Pyramid.

In a world where the Pyramid inverts, we will have Chartered Carbon Analysts roaming the world looking for the best projects, mainstream investment banks syndicating funds to support the highest-integrity projects, creative entrepreneurs inventing new ways to cut emissions cost-effectively, and a massive investment cycle in the Global South. In short, Inverting the Pyramid will deliver the scale required to impact climate change.

Instead of tearing down, it is time for the world to pull together to build the durable VCM that the planet requires.

The End

Acknowledgments

Carbon Done Correctly was inspired by my conviction that the Voluntary Carbon Market (VCM) is an essential tool in our toolbox to fight climate change. I am delighted to publicly join the overwhelming number of market participants that believe in the future of the VCM. Collectively, we are the silent majority.

One of the great thrills of completing *Carbon Done Correctly* was that I could include the names of all my friends who contributed to this effort. They and their colleagues and associates are all part of this silent majority that support the goals of the VCM. These are the builders, the believers, the entrepreneurs who understand that the VCM, when executed correctly, can be a mechanism to slow climate change and deliver benefits to disadvantaged communities.

I could not have written this book without the faithful support of Team Lawrence. I thank my wife, Dee, for perfecting the art of encouragement, criticism, and silence. Writing any book carries a cost to family members, and Dee was always willing to make the sacrifice with a smile on her face. I thank Jim Hackett for toiling through the rabbit holes and weeds of the VCM to identify that improved transparency is at the core of building trust in the VCM, and that trust is required to scale the VCM into a robust financial market. Jim is a talented writer and a soft touch to work with. I love that my books have allowed Jim to showcase his mastery of the profession. And I thank Esther Adams for cleaning up all my mixed metaphors and run-on sentences to allow *Carbon Done Correctly* to be readable, informative, and enjoyable. I would be hopeless without Esther. I was beyond fortunate when she joined my one-person office 18 years ago. Overlook Investments, Proyecto Mirador, Cool Effect and High Tide Foundation have all benefitted from her talents.

I thank Craig Pearce and the world-class team at Harriman House who made *Carbon Done Correctly* a better book. I have learned from my two books that editing is a true art form and Craig is one of the best artists of his generation. Allow me to tell one short story that captures Craig's dedication.

There is a day in every author's life when the draft manuscript arrives back from the editor. This day is preceded by weeks of worry and fear of failure. And then, one morning, the email arrives. It is one of the ultimate moments of truth.

On May 1, 2023, Craig's email arrived with the edited manuscript. My hands trembled, my breath shortened, my stomach churned as I opened the cover note. "The book is beautifully written, and it tells an incredible story." OK, every editor says this to their authors. What else did he say? "It makes me want to join you on a future trip to Honduras to see the real-life story for myself." With that comment I knew that Craig had put his heart and soul into making *Carbon Done Correctly* an interesting read. My thanks go out to all the members of Team Harriman.

I need to acknowledge the valuable contributions of Alexia Kelly. Alexia is the Voluntary Carbon Market's force of nature. She knows the methodologies, the science, the leading participants, the rabbit holes, and the 40,000-foot-high view. Readers should be thankful that Alexia joined my wife and me at High Tide Foundation early in 2023 to work on carbon policy and markets. In this role, she had the time to make a ton of valuable contributions to make the book reliable, accurate and foresightful.

I also need to acknowledge the talents of Michael and Jodi Manning, Chris Parker, and Tom Gehrig who brought the visuals of the VCM to these pages. I also thank Charlotte Boulton, for her photos of Honduras; Altaf Qadri, for his photos of India; and Regina Safri, for her photos of Indonesia. One of my objectives from the start was to make *Carbon Done*

Correctly a beautiful book and these talented folks made good on that goal. And I also must thank the group of usual suspects that fill my tank with energy. My children and their spouses: Skye and Seth; Dina and Blake; my brothers, Jim and Philip, and their families; my mother, Starr; Marisa de Belloy and all my colleagues at High Tide and Cool Effect; RC w/ DP, and all who support my efforts at Overlook and in the climate fight.

The future of the Voluntary Carbon Market is filled with uncertainty. Too often Ivory Tower academics, climate deniers and journalists look to criticize for quick publicity. Their attacks on the VCM are like so many other parts of our politicized world. We remind the naysayers that criticisms without suggested remedies are a job half done. For the rest of us, the silent majority who focus constructively on what the VCM can become, let us remember what Doña Emilia Mendoza, the Founder & Executive Director of Proyecto Mirador, told us: "When I am told that something is difficult, I've always said yes. It doesn't matter, we will do it."

Index